Bodybusiness

Originally published as
*Nonverbal Communication
for Business Success*

Ken Cooper

A Division of American Management Associations

To Sue, Jeff, and Dan

Library of Congress Cataloging in Publication Data

Cooper, Ken.
    Bodybusiness. Originally published under the title Nonverbal communication
for business success.

    Bibliography: p.
    Includes index.
    1. Success.   2. Nonverbal communication.   3. Business.   I. Title.
HF5386.C78   001.56   78-25971
ISBN 0-8144-5500-X
ISBN 0-8144-7545-0

A division of American Management Associations, New York.
All rights reserved. Printed in the United States of America.

First AMACOM paperback edition 1981

Acknowledgments

I wish to thank:

Elmer Kowal for his photographic assistance.

Monsanto Company for the use of its facilities in the photograph sessions.

Shirley Dingler for obtaining permission for the sessions.

Don Verbeck for making all session arrangements.

Jim Jones of IBM and Juanita Carter, Kathy Lowes, Dr. John Mason, Frank Miller, George Panian, Bernie Phillips, Jim Spinks, Bob Stuckey, Don Verbeck, and Iniss Taylor—all of Monsanto Company—for posing for the illustrations.

Karen Gentles for manuscript preparation.

Dr. John Gentles for thoughtful analysis of the manuscript and suggestions.

And all those friends and strangers who so graciously and patiently allowed me to experiment with them and observe them.

Preface

I always save writing the preface to a book for last. As I sit here and glance over the completed manuscript, freshly stacked in its box, I feel a strange sense of loss. *Nonverbal Communication for Business Success* contains some of my best material, up to now saved only for my consulting clients. But I feel it represents a milestone in the application of nonverbal communication to business. Nonverbal communication involves the study of all parts of the communications process *except words*—body appearance and position, body movements, possessions, surroundings, and voice characteristics. I have used nonverbal communication to advantage both in my career as a computer salesman and now as a management consultant.

There have been two main types of books about nonverbal communication: the technical research volume and the "secrets of body language" book. The technical books are filled with fascinating studies identifying behavior and causes, but they are written for the academic community in language unintelligible to the average reader. The "secrets of body language" books have been immensely popular, but they make a fatal error in assigning specific meanings to individual body signals out of context. There are a few books that present the valuable research in a readable format, and up to now no books have been designed primarily for use by the vast working public.

Nonverbal Communication for Business Success is that book. You will learn three visual "scans" that will help you systematically observe and analyze nonverbal information. The scans will enable you to determine whether many different signs *agree* before you make a decision. You can find out how to choose a restaurant for a business lunch, learn why you should look away briefly when you meet someone, and see why wearing high heels ruins your walk.

The information presented in this book is the result of nearly seven years of research into the professional literature and an equal number of years of research and experience as a teacher and management consultant. It is not an abstract theory, however; no concept has been included unless it has been proven to me in personal practice.

The book is not limited to those who work. It also contains chapters on effective voice traits and developing a successful personal image. In the chapter on image, for example, you can see how important appearance was in the 1960 and 1976 presidential debates. I have even had students use the image-building process as parents and spouses.

Now is the time for you to find out what you have been missing. Now is the time for you to transact a little "body business."

Ken Cooper

Contents

1

Nonverbal Communication and Business

It would be wonderful if a secret Eastern society existed to teach us the mysteries of effective communication. We might tear out a small coupon in the back of our favorite magazine, mail it with "only $2.99," and wait expectantly for the Ancient Wisdom Parchment to arrive.

Knowing help was on the way, we could endure our communications failures. At last, the scroll would be sure to save us. Opening the plain-wrapped package with nervous anticipation, we would finally have the answers to the most perplexing problems in human relationships.

What would the message be?

Most likely, the parchment would not offer any deep secrets to successful communication—because there are none. Instead, it would probably contain certain commonly known communications basics that researchers in the field agree on.

This book provides such basics for a special category of communications: *the nonverbals*. Much of what you read here may be intuitively obvious, some information will be new, and some will seem to contradict what you always thought to be true.

For information you already know, you will learn more effective applications. For new information, you will find that you have been watching a color TV program in black and white. Where the forest is alive with sound, you have heard only the clump of your own footsteps. For contradictions, you will experience growth in your ability to communicate effectively.

In all three cases, you will learn the *why* of communications principles. You will become a conscious participant in a process that has been a subconscious part of your behavior every waking hour. That is, you will learn to analyze the nonverbal signals being sent to you and to modify or control the nonverbal information you project.

Most people who have attained even moderate success in the business world have some ability to observe and evaluate nonverbals. For example, examine the three pictures in Figure 1–1. In each case, with whom is the salesman speaking?

A salesman in my office invariably assumed these three postures when talking on the phone, never realizing that each one indicated clearly whether or not he was working. He adopted the first pose with a customer or another employee; the second, with a friend or casual business acquaintance, such as his broker. The third was usually reserved for one of his "intimate friends," since he was a bachelor. (If you said "business associate" for the first pose and "wife" for the second, I want to know who the third person is!)

As this phone example shows, we can make fairly accurate observations in a simple social situation. In more complex settings, however, we may become confused about nonverbal signals. As a first step in overcoming this difficulty, we should examine some of the communications basics from our secret Asiatic missive.

Communications Basics

If we were holding that folded piece of paper, we would find four key concepts that can help us better understand any communications process. The first is that we communicate *with* some-

Figure 1–1. Phone conversation positions.

one, not *to* someone. Communication is not necessarily taking place just because one person is talking to another. We frequently assume that it is, until we find that our listener is a million miles away. In an article in *Reader's Digest* Carol Burnett tells such a story about a conversation with her seven-year-old daughter after a spanking:

> "At bedtime, she was still sniffling," Carol recalled. "So I went in and put my arms around her saying, 'Now, you know I love you very much.' And then I talked about character and what she did that was wrong, and she listened—never taking her eyes from my face. I began congratulating myself—boy, you are really getting through, she'll remember this when she's 40.
>
> "I talked for 20 minutes. She was spellbound; we were practically nose to nose. As I paused, searching for the clincher, she asked, 'Mommy, how many teeth do you have?'"

There's a punch, of course. The person who deserves to be punched in this type of story is frequently us. However, the humor fades when a raise is lost, a key employee quits, or a sale goes to a competitor. Communication is always a team effort between speaker and listener.

The second basic is that communication is separate from information. Communication is an *act;* information is the *content.* The medium is *not* the message, and expression of a message should not be confused with the message itself.

The third basic is that communication is nonrepeatable. There is never a chance for an identical second exchange after the first attempt. Even with writing or a film, readers or viewers change from day to day, from week to week, and are no longer the same people they were when the first exchange occurred. There is the added factor of the miscues in the first trial affecting the encore. A good example is the classic Unveiling the New Dress scene:

From the bedroom, the husband hears, "Close your eyes, hon, I want to show you something I picked up today."

If he's not thinking, the husband says, "Okay." If he's awake, he puts down his paper, mumbles a short prayer, and replies, "I'm ready!"

The rustle down the hall is punctuated by a Loretta Young

swirl as the wife asks the surely dazzled husband, "How do you like it?"

Unmoving after a short, controlled pause, he states with hopeful enthusiasm, "I really like it!"

"You don't like it! I can tell."

"No, listen, it's really a dynamite dress."

"You hate it, Harold. Any time you say 'really,' I know you're not being truthful."

"Look, what do you want me to say, 'I worship the dress'?" he replies with a rising voice. "I *like* it. I wish we had been married in it. If there was another in the store in a smaller size, I would buy it for my mother. What more do you want, a notarized oath?"

"You don't have to get sarcastic, Harold. You don't like the dress and that's all there is to it. You're never satisfied with anything I do. And speaking of your mother and a smaller size—"

"Stop! Dear, go back in the room and come out again. I *do* like the dress and I'll do whatever you want me to do."

Poor Harold isn't living in the Twilight Zone, but he might wish he were so he could get another shot at commenting on his wife's new dress. That's because communication is not repeatable. Next time, he'll be ecstatic just to protect himself. If he fumbles that opportunity, he won't get another chance then either.

The fourth communications basic is that we should consider the total message whenever we speak. People who write about NVC often promote the idea that we are continually communicating "hidden nonverbal messages" that disagree with our verbal messages. This idea may sell a lot of books and seminars, but it just isn't true. Catchphrases like "What is your body *really* saying?" and "Are you missing the opportunities on those lonely business trips?" merely titillate us. In general, there are very few discrepancies between the overall communications message and NVC. Most people just aren't good enough actors and actresses to carry it off.

As an exercise in my college classes, I have students give a two-minute talk in which all their gestures and movements conflict with what they are saying. For example, they may stomp in, slam their books to the floor, and scream in agony, "I'm glad to be here!" I limit these talks to two minutes because it takes a great deal of practice to choreograph the movements to each phrase and coordinate them in a talk.

There is a danger in taking a single NVC sign out of context. I discovered this quite by accident when I made a call on one of my regular customers, a utility executive. I naturally had tried to observe his mannerisms for any useful information, and he had one habit that drove me to distraction. Whenever I presented an idea to him, either one on one or in a presentation, he always listened with his hand covering his mouth. All the NVC literature states that this is a strong sign of disapproval or disagreement. One day while we were having a casual discussion about a communications column I wrote for a local paper, he asked me if I "used" NVC on him and if I had noticed anything unusual.

"You know, Ken," he said, "I hope I haven't given the wrong impression when I listen to you fellows. Have you noticed anything unusual about me when I listen?"

Sensing I should dig more, I said, "No, Bob. Why would you ask?"

"I read a book that told me I shouldn't put my hand over my mouth when I'm listening. Have you noticed I do this?"

"I noticed it, Bob, but I wasn't sure what it meant," I said. It *had* been bothering me, but I wasn't about to let *him* know that.

"As you can see, my face is deeply lined," he began. "I was riding the bus one day and just happened to be sitting in a seat where that large convex mirror by the rear door shot my reflection right back at me. I glanced up and saw my face looking grotesque and distorted, glaring back with an enormous frown. The lines on my face made me look terribly negative. It left such an impression on me that I decided to be certain I didn't accidentally make someone think I was angry or unhappy when I was really just listening. Now I always cover my mouth when I listen so that I won't turn the other person off."

That little confession made me breathe a sigh of sales relief. It also taught me a valuable lesson, and unlike most valuable lessons, it came relatively cheap: *No single NVC sign can be read accurately out of the context of the entire communications process.*

Nonverbal communication consists of three steps: reading, evaluating, and controlling body signals. Accurate and timely reading of nonverbal information is necessary because of the nonrepeatability of the communications process. There is no second chance. Evaluation is necessary to separate information from expression and to better identify the total message. Controlling NVC is necessary because communication is an active process, whether people are listening or speaking.

The Checklist Approach

As a firm believer in effective time management, I have written this book to be efficient and practical in its presentation of ideas. Special emphasis is given to "checklists" of nonverbal signals to help you observe and apply them in social situations. Up to now there has been no structured approach to NVC, much less to NVC in business. Yet NVC can play a major role in improving your business image and increasing your chances of success.

A WINNER WITH NVC—JOE B.

Joe B. is a prime example of how people can be winners with NVC. Before his recent retirement, Joe was one of the foremost architects in a large Midwestern city. Extremely talented, he was known as a supersalesman who always won competitive bids. This success was especially remarkable in view of the way organizations select architects. When a company decides to go out for bids, it will schedule marathon sessions during which any qualified architect, solicited or otherwise, is allowed to present ideas. On the appointed day the architects assemble outside the conference room like a bevy of shotputters, flexing their muscles and trying to psych out their opponents. They sit with their drawings rolled up under their arms and nervously wait their turn.

Joe's success was so legendary that when he merely walked into the waiting area, half the architects immediately got up and left without presenting. Joe was an exceptional architect, but he was not that far ahead of his rivals in technical skills. What gave Joe the edge was his superiority in communications skills. He was so superior, in fact, that his competitors began to assume he would win.

In a long conversation with Joe one sunny afternoon, I asked him about his secret. He had a very simple method. "When I go into the room," he said, "I look for two people. The first is the Star, the big boss. He is the key decision maker. I make certain I sell to him and get his commitment. I also look for the Heel. This is the negative guy, the one who will make trouble for me when I present and when I'm out of the room. I make sure I either put him in his place or draw out his criticisms so I can respond to them before I leave."

"It all sounds simple enough," I commented, eager for some juicy tips, "but how do you tell who is the Heel or Star?"

Giving the answer I feared, he responded, "Oh, you can just tell."

Therein lies the excitement of NVC—and the frustration. NVC can increase your chances of business success, but only if you have a systematic technique for learning its vocabulary and applying it in business. The NVC checklists in the first three chapters of this book will give you a framework for learning the vocabulary you need. The three NVC checklists follow the standard pattern of observation: where you put your body, its appearance and what you put around it, and what you do with it once it is there. The remaining chapters will help you gain fluency.

1. **Body Position and Status**	Territorial space
	Height might
	Tread spread
	Size prize
	Seating dynamics
	Office etiquette
2. **Indicators**	Personal
	Shared
	Public
3. **Body Movement**	Center
	Head
	Posture
	Hands
	Legs

With practice, you will be able to make these NVC scans automatically, taking only a few moments to size up a new person or situation. The time is always available, even if you are speaking. Scientists estimate the speed of conversational thought at 750 words per minute; yet average speech is only 150 words per minute. This leaves you with 80 percent of your mental capacity to do other things. Frequently, you may daydream or plan your next response with this time. What you ought to do is become a better "listener" with your eyes.

NVC in Business

You may be curious about how much information you will gain if your eyes do become better listeners. Albert Mehrabian conducted a series of tests to determine how much body, voice, and words contributed to the communication of attitudes. Take a moment to fill in your estimates of the proper percentages. (Remember, the percentages should reflect the communication of *attitudes*, not ideas.)

BODY	%
VOICE	%
WORDS	%
	100 %

The results of Mehrabian's research were body, 55 percent; voice, 38 percent; and words, 7 percent. The percentages are, of course, highly dependent on the situation measured. After asking my audiences this question for seven years, I obtained the following averages: body, 60 percent; voice, 30 percent; and words, 10 percent. Our attitudes are communicated silently. This is the message that most people miss.

If you don't agree with my percentages—if you believe that words are far more important—you can do a little research on your own. Try this experiment when you come home from work tomorrow. As you walk in, tell your loved ones that you do, indeed, love them. Run over to them, shake your fist, and sweetly say, "I love you!" Then walk away snarling, with a horrible grimace on your face, while you clench and unclench your fists. If words are truly more important than gestures, your loved ones will come over to you with outstretched arms and sweetly respond, "Why, thank you, honey. What a nice surprise. We love you too."

If you survived that experiment, you can follow up with a test on words versus tone of voice. When you come home from work *two* days from now, wait for your loved one to ask, "How was your day, dear?" Then walk over, maintaining as pleasant an expression as possible, and say in a loud voice, "I had just a wonderful day!" with as much sarcasm as you can muster. Once again, if the response is anything other than "That's nice, dear," voice is the dominant factor. Your experiments will have to stop here if you don't want your loved one to develop a nervous tic when you arrive home. If the responses were calm and oriented solely to your words, you can forget this book. You've somehow landed Mr. Spock from *Star Trek*.

President Franklin Roosevelt was particularly aware of NVC. Standing in a boring receiving line one evening, he decided to have a little fun. As each guest came up and said, "Good evening, Mr. President, how are you, sir?" he responded warmly with a pleasant smile, "Fine, thank you, I just murdered my mother-in-law." Not one person going through the receiving line reacted to his comment. It's doubtful people even heard it.

You are now ready to flex your communications muscles at the office. As you walk down the hall tomorrow, try an FDR. When you're asked, "Howya doin'?" cheerfully bubble, "Pretty bad, and you?" Keep count of how many of your fellow workers even hear your words. If *anybody* hears them, he or she is unusually attentive. Most of those you meet will be paying attention only to your nonverbals.

Obviously, words are important and necessary for conveying *ideas* or detailed information. If that weren't true, this book might be a film. (Not a bad idea!) In general, your body is the best indicator of *purpose* and your voice is the best indicator of *importance*.

NVC AND SUCCESS

NVC has an important impact on all of us. Every President since John F. Kennedy has been tutored in NVC. These politicians realized the tremendous effect of NVC on people's perception of a candidate and on their voting decisions. Your NVC can drastically affect the decisions of your voters—those people in authority who hold your career in their hands.

The animal kingdom, dealing with its human masters, is much more successful than most of us are in using NVC. Even the youngest members are quite adept at seeing into us. If you have ever trained a puppy, you've seen an advanced NVC-reading organism at work.

When you train a puppy, sooner or later you find a "mistake of the second kind" (solid). As you're kneeling there in resigned disgust, your nice canine bumbles by. You call it, using your kindest, sweetest doggy voice. "Here, Thorndyke! Come here, sweet puppykins. Your faithful and kind owner wants to pet your lovable doggy hide."

Does Thorndyke come? Of course not! He knows full well that you plan to beat the daylights out of him with today's news, slam his nose in what he did, and throw him out in the cold, lonely backyard. He knows because he can read your NVC even though you were trying to appear as kind and nice as possible. You even reinforced his feelings by carrying the paper in your hand.

The first recorded NVC professional was not even human. He was a wizard by the name of Clever Hans who could perform *any* mathematical computation at all. Hans was a horse who lived in Germany in the early 1900s, touring the countryside and giving sellout performances at each stop. He would answer any question from the audience that could be represented by the tapping of a hoof. For a year and a half, audiences were baffled, swearing that there had to be a trick. The show conditions got tougher and tougher, but Hans never missed a question.

Then, after 18 months of success, Hans flopped for the first time. He missed a question that was asked by someone out of his line of sight and kept secret from his trainer. Clever Hans's hoof tapped right past the correct answer. For the first time in his career, Clever Hans was no longer clever.

The reason was simple. On his own, Hans had learned that if he stopped tapping his hoof at a certain point, he would get a reward. Hans was nothing more than a psychologist's rat responding to a stimulus. The stimulus Hans responded to was the tension in his trainer! He found that if he stopped tapping just as the tension eased—that is, just when he had tapped out the answer—he was rewarded. When the question was given to him from someone out of his sight, and kept secret from the trainer, there was no tension to "read."

Hans made his career from NVC, and so have many others in various ways, like Joe B. You too have the talent and the ability—if you just take the time to learn the vocabulary of NVC —to improve your business image by bettering your communications skills. For the first time in your life, you will have the knowledge to interpret some of the massive nonverbal data that used to be summarily shunted to the brain's roundfile. It's time you added the title Nonverbal Communicator to your business credentials.

2

Relative
Body Location

Our language recognizes the importance of NVC with such body-oriented phrases as:

Cold shoulder	Face up to it
Shake it off	Chin up
Get it off your chest	Grit your teeth
Stiff upper lip	Shoulder a burden
At arm's length	Glad-hander

These phrases are almost more than we can swallow. You've got to hand it to me, though, the ones I dug up are real eye-openers. I can keep them coming hand over fist, until your knees buckle. But don't let your spirits droop; I promise to quit slinging these out before you turn your back in disgust.

The term *body language,* popularized by Julius Fast in his book of the same name, refers to the portion of NVC relating solely to physical communication, excluding voice. Body language is actually the study of three concepts: proxemics, indicators, and kinesics. *Proxemics* (derived from the Greek word meaning "to approach") covers the analysis of body locations. *Indicators,* a sociological term, refers to the objects we gather around us. *Kinesics* is the study of physical movements.

In coming chapters we will not only examine these three areas, but also cover vocal traits, environment, and image as key nonverbal signals of attitude. This chapter introduces the checklist for evaluating body position and status:

> Territorial space
> Height might
> Tread spread
> Size prize
> Seating dynamics
> Office etiquette

Territorial Space

The first questions you should ask yourself in any business situation is "Where are people located and why are they there?" The distance we maintain with others is related to our feelings toward them and indicates something about our relationships. This distance is called *territorial space*. There are four basic zones of territorial space: intimate, personal, social, and public.

INTIMATE SPACE

Intimate space includes distances up to about one and a half feet. It is used for such activities as lovemaking, comforting, protecting, and family greeting. It is also used for wrestling, basketball, sitting in movie theaters, and standing in elevators or on crowded streetcorners. Intimate space is usually reserved for people who have the right to be that close to us. Such familiarity and relaxation of normal distances most often require time and a deepening of relationships. Sometimes this is not always possible, as in an elevator, where closeness to strangers makes most of us feel uncomfortable.

The importance of maintaining my own intimate space was brought home to me one afternoon. A salesman and I were having a casual conversation about the poor economy when I began to get nervous. The salesman kept shifting closer to me as we talked, stopping at a distance of a foot, which put our faces all of nine inches apart. I decided to try a little experiment, partly out of interest and mostly out of self-preservation.

Fortunately, we were at his desk, out in the middle of a large room, so I had plenty of space to work with. As we talked, I slowly backed around the desk, leaning forward all the while to "wean" him off my face. As I stood upright, he unconsciously took a step around the desk, and I was back in his clutches. I performed the maneuver again, so that I was now on the opposite side of the desk from where we started, but the results were the same. I was trapped!

Deciding it was time for more serious measures, I slowly shifted around him and eased over to our starting point, leaning over the desk until I arrived. When I stood upright, he immediately walked around the desk without slowing his conversation. In what I thought to be a flash of brilliance, I sat on the desk so I could put my knees between us. When he moved to stand between my legs, I became desperate. In a last-ditch effort, I leaned back on my hands as I sat. He then leaned forward until I yelled, "Stop! I give up! I give up! You win!"

"What do you mean?" was the quizzical, unmoving reply.

"Don't move a muscle, Mike," I said, as I put my thumb on my nose and touched his nose with the little finger of the same hand. "You're just too damn close for my personal comfort! You are only *that* far away from my face," I said, showing him my outstretched hand. "My *wife* and I don't even converse at this distance!"

"Well, that's your problem, Cooper!" he returned, stomping off in a huff. Later Mike came back to me and mentioned that several customers he had asked admitted they felt as I did. You can't use intimate space unless you have earned the right to be there.

Police purposely use space invasion. One of my students, a county police officer, talked about using this approach in questioning suspects. Leaning forward, he would draw his chair up to the seated suspect until his knee touched the chair between the suspect's knees. He and the other officers would trade off the questioning stints, never letting the suspect regain his territorial space. As the officer put it, "Who needs rubber hoses when I can crowd them as long as I like?"

Personal Space

Personal space includes distances of one to two and a half feet. Personal distance is normally maintained between two friends in conversation—for example, at a small lunchroom table. Office workers standing around the water cooler will often maintain this distance, as will people at a cocktail party who know each other. Reduce the distance to intimate space, and your acquaintance will become very uncomfortable, most likely moving away to restore the personal space.

One of the oddities of TV is that the actors often have to talk almost nose to nose to be included in a closeup shot. A humorous example is the "medicinal elixir" commercial where a pleasant young couple stands against a black backdrop and the husband says something like, "This is my wife and I love her. Because she knows she's important, she takes Killital to maintain our love." The ridiculous part of this commercial is that the man and woman are right on top of each other. He is breathing hotly on her forehead and she is craning her neck to smile and look up to him with love. Real people, no matter how intimate, do not talk to each other three inches apart. Even at rip-roaring drunken brawls, at least personal distance is maintained (for conversation, naturally).

Social Space

Social space is approximately four to seven feet. Phrases such as "stand back so I can see you" and "keep him at arm's length" reflect our need for social space. In business, the prime protector of social space is the desk. It automatically puts the heads of the people seated on either side about seven feet apart. The same goes for a conference table, dining table, or counter in a store. Studies of trends in office furniture have shown that status-conscious top executives are getting rid of their desks, files, and drawers, figuring they are above all that. But they are replacing their desks with tables of approximately the same size, in order to maintain control of the social space around their chair.

Strangers thrown together at a party will initially form circles of social space. At social gatherings I often try to determine who already knows whom and who just met by observing how far apart people are standing.

Recently I had a half-hour discussion with a man who knew I was an NVC consultant. He spent the time arguing that NVC is hokum and a complete waste of time. I was happy to let him ramble, because as we were talking I moved closer and then farther away. He unconsciously shifted his position to maintain his own comfortable social space. In the course of the conversation, we meandered up and down a hall and in and out of two offices, ending up where the hall met the office areas. After he finished one particularly long tirade, I said, "Look, I'll buy what you said about NVC if you can answer one simple question for me."

"Sure," he sneered. "What is it?"

"Tell me," I returned, "why have you and I been in and out of a hall and two offices at least twice in the past half-hour?"

He stared at me for a moment and stomped off. I may not have gained a convert, but I won an argument nonverbally.

Public Space

Public space, usually ten feet or more, is reserved for strangers whom we don't care to notice or interact with. People waiting in the lobby for an elevator will mill about at this distance. Even on a busy streetcorner people will try to maintain this space. Watch public places such as lobbies, transportation terminals, reception areas, and museums for how strangers maintain public space.

The importance of public space was illustrated by an experiment performed at a college library. A graduate assistant went to the library when it was relatively empty and purposely sat at an occupied table. Responses varied from complete indifference, to dirty looks, to disgusted stares. Yet in 80 trials, only one person asked her to move. The assistant finally asked to be replaced in the experiment because the subjects in the library made her feel so guilty for intruding.

CONTROLLING TERRITORIES

There is a wealth of information to be gained from observing how attendees mill about before a meeting or "shoot the breeze" around the cooler. It is easy to determine which person is the leader in a group. When a superior is talking with a number of subordinates, the configuration often takes on a "choir effect," as shown in Figure 2–1. The leader, at the top of the diagram, is given more space; the others are facing the leader in a semicircle. The "choir" will usually stand attentively, rarely turning to leave unless someone else arrives to fill the gap.

In a leaderless group, it is apparent who is "in" or "out" by their physical position. In Figure 2–1 the person on the lower left has walked up to a conversation and been recognized but not

Figure 2–1. Standing positions.

admitted to the group. Notice how the two people on either side of the newcomer have created a small gap, but not enough to give the newcomer equal space. All of us have been in this predicament at one time or another and often walk away with no small feeling of rejection.

The territorial space characteristics of an office are indicative of its owner. An executive may want to crowd visitors to his or her office by placing the desk about a third of the way between the door and the back wall. This way, the executive has ample space to lean away from the desk, put his feet up, or swivel. The visitor has little space, which connotes less importance or dominance. A client of mine laid out his office in this manner. He placed a large tree on the visitor's side, so that there was just enough room between the desk, tree, and wall for a chair. I can't cross my legs in the chair, much less be comfortable. Of course, my client always apologizes for the smallness of the office, but I've heard he has had the opportunity to move and has refused several times.

The amount of available space can also affect the success of a meeting. I always avoid a small classroom in my training sessions, because the audience is much more argumentative and harder to control. The same holds true for a business meeting. If there is not enough space for the participants, the meeting has a much smaller chance for success as time passes.

We often use objects to mark our territorial space, much as a dog "anoints" a new backyard to indicate its territory. People sitting on a bus or plane will fill the other seat with their belongings to "claim" the space. On the *Tonight Show*, actress Angie Dickinson mentioned that she prefers to read during a flight rather than talk to other passengers. So she always puts her carry-on luggage and accessories in the seat next to her until right before departure to discourage anyone from sitting there. Walls can also be used to define territorial space. Members of a department will fill the walls within their boundaries with pictures, contest posters, or other paraphernalia to indicate the department's physical territory.

Sometimes, we have to claim our territory personally. At a "husbands and wives too" office party, an executive I know was having an animated conversation with his young secretary. They were sitting on the couch and she was touching his arm as they talked, holding his eyes with a steady gaze. Suddenly his wife came over, sat down beside him, smoothed his collar, and listened without saying a word. The move was a show of possession, reminding the secretary of the wife's "territory." The message was not lost on the secretary, because the conversation ended soon afterwards and was not resumed that evening.

Men use the same sort of maneuver at social gatherings to demonstrate possession of their wives or women friends. A man comes up to his woman and casually slips an arm around her waist. In effect, he is saying to the other man, "She's mine, remember?"

Territorial space can be manipulated to gain control, as in the police interrogation example described above. Intruding on people's space is one of the most common forms of domination in business. Some people can make us feel like a rabbit at the wolves' convention by talking close to us, as Mike did. The effect can be intensified by offensive personal habits. If you have a tough meeting coming up, schedule it in a small conference room and anticipate it with a big, garlic lunch. Rope-sized cigars made from buffalo chips are another executive weapon in the discomfort race. Chest poking (the female version is arm punching), nudging (remember Monty Python's "Nudge, Nudge" sketch?), and backslapping are further insults to our sense of space. After 20 minutes of one of the above, most of us are ready to agree to almost anything.

If you want to hold an efficient, spirited meeting, keep the space tight. This can help shorten the duration better than any schedule. Small spaces also intensify conflict. In making recommendations to management negotiators at a large chemical plant, I suggested that they meet with the union local in a "cozy" little conference room. This was to take advantage of the well-known antagonism between the young union president and an old-line vice-president. Although the negotiating sessions were prolonged, the union's inability to present a united front was beneficial to the company.

If you wish to reduce conflict in a session, provide more space. Spread everyone out around a large table in a spacious room.

Become aware of others' needs for territorial space. By moving closer or farther away during a conversation, see if you can determine the space your business associates and acquaintances require. As you grow more familiar with the uses of territorial space, you will be able to continue conversations others are trying to break off by keeping within conversational distance. (I have moved with people as much as 50 feet in a ten-minute chat they wished to break off.) You will learn to stay farther away from people who are trying to control you and to get closer to those you wish to dominate. You will discover that territorial space is both an indicator and a tool in effective NVC.

Height Might

Height has long been associated with the desirable, with success. Up is good and down is bad. Our language is full of phrases like "look up to him," "raised to peerage," "put on a pedestal," "on top of the world," "rise to the occasion," and "high and mighty." No self-respecting god would ever be caught down low, in Death Valley or the Bonneville Salt Flats. They live in places like Mt. Olympus and Valhalla.

Height is a symbol of power and superiority. The winner stands highest on the Olympic awards platform. A judge's courtroom bench is always elevated. Victorious football players put the coach on their shoulders and carry him off the field. Raymond Burr (as Perry Mason) never went up to the judge's bench to argue an objection. How could he appear intimidating if he stood there like a youngster filching cookies off the counter? That was okay for a little villain like Hamilton Burger, but not for our Perry!

Lack of height has always been a sign of inferiority. We can "fall short" of a goal, "think small," be "shortsighted," or be "looked down on." Being lower is a sign of servility. In ancient

Figure 2–2. Height might.

(Copyright © 1977 King Features Syndicate Inc.)

times, vanquished soldiers were forced to pass under a chest-high arch of spears in front of the conquering general. Anyone who refused to bow down was allowed to wear a spear home, buried in his chest. Even today we don't like anyone to "lord it over us."

We consistently favor people with a height advantage, as Figure 2–2 shows. In this century only two presidential candidates who were shorter than their opponents have been elected, and these only recently in the times of TV campaigning. The first was Richard Nixon (5′11½″) "over" George McGovern (6′1″); the second was Jimmy Carter (5′9½″) "over" Gerald Ford (6′1″). Business also rewards height. A 1972 study of University of Pittsburgh graduates showed that those in the 6′2″ to 6′4″ range received 12% higher starting salaries than their fellow graduates, independent of any other factors.

The dominance of height is no secret to today's business executive. Everyone knows the importance of standing up to address a meeting in order to gain control.

Many executives choose their office furniture so they can dominate visitors. They sit on large, high-backed, elevated desk chairs while offering their visitors low-slung lounge chairs that are almost impossible to get out of, much less sit up in. A woman who runs a very successful resume service has an office designed this way. Many clients have complained about the low chairs and her obvious attempt to dominate with height. But she denies any purpose to the layout, claiming she merely used the furniture that was available to her. It is interesting to note, however, that despite client complaints she hasn't changed anything.

You can't saw the legs off of someone who is taller than you or modify your office furniture in secret, but there are ways to minimize a height disadvantage. This is particularly important to women in business, since women as a group are shorter than men. As I pointed out in the section on territorial space, distance is a good counteragent for domination. A 6'4" executive who is overwhelming up close is almost completely neutralized at public distances. Sitting at opposite ends of the table, talking from the door of his office, and getting up and moving while you talk will all help you stay even.

A 5'9" IBM sales training manager claimed that he could minimize height might in tough sales calls on any tall executives. Just when the customer was bearing down the hardest, leaning over the desk and slamming points home, the manager would get up and walk over to a window and begin gazing out thoughtfully. He would continue the conversation with, "Now, you've made several good points here. Let me see if I understand them." As he restated the customer's position, occasionally glancing back toward the desk, the customer would often calm down and begin to agree or amplify. Sometimes the customer would even follow him to the window. Then the conversation would continue more rationally as both men pondered the outdoors. Only when the meeting was back on an even basis would the manager return to his chair, successful in escaping a tough situation.

Another way to minimize height differences is to carefully control the location of any conversation or meeting. Like the spider, you should conduct business safely in your web—the office. Adjust the height of your desk chair if needed. Find visitors' chairs that are soft and comfortable, but not so low as to be obvious. Some executives have even had hidden platforms constructed behind their desks. Make your office the one place where you can be in control. Save important conversations for times when you can invite your boss in as he is walking by your door. If he's smart, he'll suggest you follow him to his office. If he's not, you can trap him in yours by saying, "I've got something important to discuss with you," and walking over and closing the door. Once that door is shut, he's psychologically locked in.

When you can't arrange a conversation in your office, at least hold it outside of your associate's office. Talk over lunch if you must. It is almost impossible for an associate to be domineering when special sauce is running out the corner of his mouth or when he's munching a hard luncheon roll with crumbs bouncing from plate to lap. In addition, being in public limits the tactics your associate can use. Other places where height advantage is relatively meaningless are in a car or airplane, in a bar or lounge with deep chairs, and in a crowd.

Being outnumbered also tends to neutralize height might. One of my former managers used to crowd subordinates into his small office for weekly team meetings. I made a point of coming in last when all the chairs were taken. The only spot left was a heater module, which was about desk high and somewhat behind the manager's chair. When I sat on it I was head and shoulders above him and to his rear. The first few meetings I did this he was slightly uneasy but accepted my excuse about no place to sit. The third meeting he *ordered* me to get a chair. This still wasn't acceptable, because he was surrounded. Even if he had stood up, his height dominance would have affected only the people he was facing. He could not address the people at his sides without twisting like a physical fitness expert. This "screaming Mongolian horde" approach can help you make up in numbers what you may lack in physical size.

A final approach to minimizing height advantages is to act aggressively. An administrator in a sales office felt he was being treated unfairly, but he knew he would be lost if he went in to talk with the office manager. The manager was a tall man and a smooth, persuasive talker. Deciding on an aggressive approach, the administrator worked himself into a suitable "mad" and stormed into the office. He strode up to the manager's desk and began telling him what was wrong, pounding the desk to emphasize his points. This continued for a few minutes until the manager slipped in during a pause and said, "Jack, Jack! Sit down and we'll talk about it."

Jack responded with, "I can't sit down, I'm too upset!" and continued to talk. The manager finally broke loose from the onslaught by standing up, at which point Jack abruptly said, "I'm sorry I've gotten so worked up. We'll have to talk about it when I get myself calmed down," and walked out to lunch. The story ended happily when the problem was later resolved, which Jack insists was due solely to his aggressive tactics.

If you are among those of us who won't be getting that 12% higher starting salary, you now have several techniques to use against those who will. Being "one up" is often little more than being physically up, a situation you can handle by using the information in this chapter to "stand tall" with others.

Tread Spread

A variation on height dominance, and the third item on the body position and status checklist, is walking position. Like being "on top," being a "front-runner" is an indicator of status and power. (Why else do we speed up when a VW tries to pass?) In a military inspection, the highest-ranking reviewing officer always walks in front. In a procession of royalty, the monarch is always at the head. I have never seen a picture of former President Ford and former Secretary Kissinger when Kissinger was not sensitive enough to remain in the background. In pictures of Kissinger with his wife, Nancy, she is usually behind her husband. (After all, "*behind* every successful man, there is a woman.") Some cultures require people of lower status to walk at least one step behind their superiors. State department officials closely examine all photos showing dignitaries of "closed" countries such as Russia and China. In pictures of a group walking, power or status is shown by how near the front of the pack an individual is.

Can you imagine the top executive of your organization walking down the hall leaning over your boss's shoulder? Ridiculous. Yet the chances are you've seen a subordinate of the executive walking in that position. One of my students, a bank vice-president, remarked, "So that's why I always end up walking through the bank sideways like a sand crab, talking to one of my people. I've even mentioned it to a few of them, but we still end up this way.''

Observe walking position in meeting a new group or sitting in a strange office. I used to watch groups of my customers come out of the elevator, walk up to the reception desk, then arrange themselves around the sign-in table. The boss would usually lead the way. In the instances where he trailed, the others would wait for him to do the talking and sign in first. If one person defers and lets another go ahead, that is further proof of status. An underling does not usually defer to the boss; the boss goes ahead as a matter of course. The subordinate never had the privilege of being ahead in the first place!

I'm frequently asked, ''What about a man who opens the door for a woman? What does that mean?'' With many men, this is merely a courtesy. In a *business situation*, it is an acknowledgment of dominance. Ignoring the differences in sex, wouldn't you be nervous if, during a long stroll through your office building, your boss carefully opened *each* door for you? You might think, ''I've got to stop letting him do this. He'll think I'm lazy or insensitive!'' You end up rushing to the next door to usher him in first so that you don't get too far into his psychological debt—the position a woman is in by continuously accepting this ''courtesy.''

It's time to step out and become a front-runner. One of the hardest things to do is to take initiative. Foursomes bumble at the reservations desk, indecisive about which couple should ask for the reservations. If we are in between two others walking along the street and are forced to crowd down to two wide because of people coming the other way, we are the ones who step into the evasive tap dance trying to save our shins as we fall behind. We are part of that pack milling around the reception desk or hesitating self-consciously at a doorway.

New Yorkers never hesitate. If you stand in front of a pedestrian in New York, you will go home with hundreds of footprints on your body. In the Midwest I did the face-to-face dance many times in order to get by someone coming toward me. Now, when faced with someone coming directly at me, I stop and let the other person move aside or alter his course.

In your office, stop walking behind your bosses. Stay even, or walk in front of them occasionally. Women, open the door for men as the opportunity arises. You may earn a few "libber" grumbles, but if you make the gesture matter-of-factly, the comments will die down. These little changes in walking position can go a long way in building confidence and showing your power. If "it's what's up front that counts," then you had better get there and stay there!

Size Prize

Another variation on height might is size prize, or physical bulk. Our society idolizes size. The most obvious obsession is with the female figure. Ever since an image was first captured on film, America has made a succession of no-talent "femmes énormales" famous and rich. The Playboy empire was dedicated to ferreting out "les glandes grandes." No wonder some women risk serious medical complications to be enhanced by silicone. Size and success are nearly synonymous.

One of my customers, a small airlines company, had the usual flight attendant training system in its home office. It never ceased to amaze me that, while it took a memo three days to go across the hall, it took only 30 minutes for the whole company (male and female) to know that there was a top-heavy young beauty in the current crop of trainees. Mondays at the training area were always busy enough, but once the word leaked out there was a never ending stream of employees just "going by" at break time. Let the poor young woman venture out of the training nest, and the carpets would practically wear out as she stood there.

The respect and love of bigness is *everywhere*. My son watches a Saturday morning cereal commercial that praises the stuff solely for its size. A group of kids in a beat-up wooden hideout sing, "Honeycrumb's big. Big, BIg, BIG! Got a big bite. Right, RIGht, RIGHT! Honeycrumb's a big mouthful, it tastes just right!" Who cares if it's nutritional or if it tastes like outdoor rug glue, as long as it fills up your mouth?

Many consumer products focus on bigness. If your soap isn't

selling, bring it out in a new, larger container. The words "big" and "large" have become so overworked that companies have come up with "family size" and "industrial size" just to announce even more bigness. After all, where else but in America could a fast-food franchise succeed on the strength of a product named the Whopper?

Movies also have to be big. Papers are filled with ads like:

> See *Tidal Jaws: The Towering Earthquake Adventure, 1932.* With a cast of billions. See the destruction of the entire earth in Sound-abound. Feel, breathe the panoramic majesty of massive death. Thrill to the biggest galaxy of stars since the Crab Nebula in a glut of cameo roles. Watch as Ralph, the mechanical earth, a 100 percent scale model, self-destructs, bringing the entire studio down with it.

Even our activities have to be big. "This is the biggest thing that ever happened to this town." One of the most popular books last year was a collection of world records on "the biggest." Heavyweights are the only boxers most sports fans follow. Even the most ardent collegiate football fan probably has no idea that there is a lightweight football league in the Northeast.

Physical bulk is an enormous advantage in today's business world. Several years ago, my office had a chance to interview the graduating captain of Notre Dame's football team. Even though he was a fine offensive tackle, he felt he would have a hard time making it in the pros, so he was interviewing for a position through the college placement office. He was a giant—your average, run-of-the-mill Notre Dame offensive lineman. To his credit (and against his stereotype), he owned a high gradepoint average and had excellent leadership qualities. But what do you think the comments from management were?

"Did you see that guy we had in here today? He could have bent my arm with one hand and tossed me through the window with a flick of the wrist! And he's even qualified."

"Man, if we land that hulk, we'll have a real superstar on our hands."

"He can't miss. Can you imagine letting him call on (customer name deleted)? He'd eat that little pipsqueak alive."

To the football player's credit, he turned down a very lucrative offer, one, I suspect, higher than any other trainee received. For some reason, everyone in the office acted as if we still carry clubs. Evidently we do, only they are psychological clubs.

Remember the University of Texas football slogan of the late 1960s? "If you've got it, flaunt it!" If you are blessed with physical size (not fat, we'll discuss that later), maximize its effect. Maintain closer territorial spaces, dwarf everything you come in contact with. Have a smaller desk and keep the chairs tightly grouped. If you have a large office, jam the furniture into one small area and decorate the empty space or turn it into an unused "casual setting."

Emphasize your physical bulk. Give iron handshakes, talk loudly, slap backs, and punch shoulders. Tell people you play in an adult hockey league for the physical contact. Rugby is even better. (Every rugby player I ever met thought a minor injury was one where you could at least get up before the game was over. A major injury has never been defined.)

One of my customers was an enormous man who would rather crush your hand than look at you. Though I have a fairly large, powerful hand, I was still on the edge of agony every time I greeted him. I was careful to remove my college ring before making any calls on him. He had the habit of pulling his hand back slightly so that my knuckles were in his grasp and my second and fourth fingers were crushed against the unyielding ring. It was impossible to be assertive with this man while nursing a mutilated paw.

Another man in our office let it be known that he had been a heavyweight boxing champion in his youth and used to earn extra money by staying in the ring three rounds with carnival knockout artists. He managed to get into a bar fight every year or so to reinforce his reputation. All he had to do at a meeting was to begin to get a little agitated or start pounding the table, and the others would back off. Although there had never been the hint of a disturbance in his business career, he used this veiled threat successfully for years.

If you are small or slight, you can minimize your lack of size by manipulating your environment. Get a massive desk. Use large, high-armed, heavy office chairs that cannot be moved easily and place them slightly away from your desk. Large bookshelves, enormous paintings, giant displays or charts, all serve to minimize size differences between people. Imagine two men standing under the Gateway Arch in St. Louis, one is 6'4" and the other 5'8". Size becomes unimportant because they are both dwarfed by their surroundings.

Don't worry about drawing attention to your size with this approach, particularly if you have a large office. If your office is small, use lighting to help achieve the same effect. Don't use bright ceiling lights. Take out several ceiling bulbs at night if you have to. Keep the room a comfortable brightness, like a family room, and use an attractive desk lamp for working. Bright light brings out the details of size, making a room and everything in it look smaller. Softer lighting minimizes any negative feature, such as a bad paint job or worn furniture. The more ornate and impressive your trappings are, the less your physical bulk will matter. Is it any wonder that the mousy boss Mr. Foofram in the "Hi and Lois" comic strip has a big, fancy office?

The key to overcoming lack of size is to battle the problem subtly. Small people in business face a strange double bind. If they are aggressive and successful, they are accused of having a Napoleon complex; they are "overcompensating." Remarks such as "She's a tiger for such a little girl" and "He's a real bantam rooster" abound. These are negative compliments of the worst kind. If small people are organization-minded, compliant, and helpful, they are regarded as poor little folks who never made up for size. The truly successful small person in business must develop a style that does not let the question of size ever become a concern. Even if some of the funds must come from your own pocket, make your office the one place where your personal features are maximized. Don't go in for elevator shoes or a Napoleon personality. Let competence speak for you.

One of the most dynamic small people I have ever met also has one of the best corporate styles I have ever seen. He started as the proprietor of a small hardware store and built it into a chain of retail sales and rental stores. After retiring at 32 for two years, he decided to re-enter business and is now vice-president of a large construction firm. If you are familiar with the construction industry, you know it has the biggest collection of hardnosed, burly brutes in the working world. There is no room for the meek

or mild. But this executive has the complete respect and cooperation of everyone who works for him. I have never heard any of
the short-guy putdowns, nor have I heard any Napoleon remarks.
He works with overwhelming, inarguable competence. He never
has to raise his voice. He never makes rash judgments. Because
there is so little doubt about him as a businessman, there is also
little doubt about him as a man. True competence, controlled
competence, is the only way to escape the small person double
bind.

A woman in business faces the same sort of problem. She
may have to deal not only with an inferiority in bulk but also with
an attitude of "natural inferiority" ingrained in her male associates. Her double bind is that of being "just a woman" or, if she
begins to succeed, of being a "pushy broad," who is trying to
become "one of the boys." The answer for her is the same as for
the small businessman: competence.

One of my evening college students was a department manager in a large retail store. Only 21 years of age, she was the first
"executive level" manager ever to reach that position without a
college degree. A tall, imposing young woman, I asked her secret.

"I was very lucky when I was younger," she revealed,
"because both my parents were imposing and thought I would be
too. They made a point of making me proud of my size, even
during those years when being large was the dating kiss of death.
So many of my female friends who are large slump and act
ashamed of what should be an advantage."

As an experiment, I included this question on the classes'
midterm exam: "How should a large woman manage her proxemics (body location) for maximum effect?" Four out of six women
and all seven men in the class assumed that she should *de-empha-
size* her size advantage. If you are blessed with natural size advantages, don't make the same mistake. You've got it; use it!

Seating Dynamics

Ever since Howard and Cosell, the first two cavemen with
the dawning of intelligence in their eyes, decided that there must
be something better than working doubled up on the ground like a

duck, people have vied for status through seating position. How-ard probably found a flat-sided rock and rolled it over to the cave for Cosell to see (which is not easy to do with a flat-sided rock, but then again they were cavemen). One of them, undoubtedly Cosell, suddenly had the bright idea of laying it flat side *up*, and in a flash the table was born. The little scene surely ended with an argument over who would get to sit at the narrow end of the rock.

The locations we choose for sitting are loaded with nonver-bal data. Remember the Paris peace talks on ending the Vietnam war? Diplomats spent several *years* trying to determine the seat-ing arrangements for the various delegates. Seating arrangements are no less important in business.

ASSOCIATION APPROXIMATION

Certain seating positions are conducive to different types of interaction. By observing those positions, we can begin to draw fairly accurate conclusions about relationships. Figure 2–3 shows four variations in seating dynamics.

Cooperation is best when people are sitting next to each other. When a teacher is tutoring a student or an office worker is showing a replacement how to do a certain job, they usually sit next to each other so both can work from the same document.

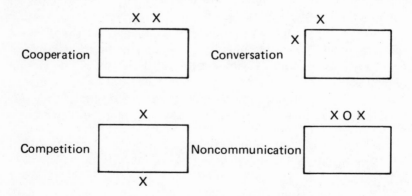

Figure 2–3. Sitting positions.

Conversation is facilitated when people are sitting at adjacent corners of a table. The company lunchroom is a good place to observe this. (If the table is small, though, conversation may be uncomfortable because of insufficient territorial space. In this case, the two people will sit across from each other.) Conversation requires closeness, but not to the same degree as sharing reading material.

Competitors often confront each other face to face, like Western gunslingers. Opponents in a meeting tend to sit across the table from each other, either at the middle or at each end. This way, each one can "keep an eye on" the other. Their underlings or support personnel frequently choose the seats on either side of their "gunslinger," much like lining up for the showdown at the corral. If there is to be no fight, the opponents may choose the noncommunication position, with someone sitting between them. The more people between them, the harder it is to converse. The effect is similar to trying to talk to a relative at the Thanksgiving table with a hearty eater bobbing up and down between you. You end up leaning back and forth like an antenna in the carwash.

TABLE STATUS

You should be familiar with the dominant and subordinate positions around a rectangular business meeting table. The dominant positions are the ends. The middle of the table is a secondary dominant position and is usually used for active defense or for disagreement with the leader on the end. The weakest positions are in between the powers, in the "dead zone" of status.

The first table in Figure 2–4 shows the normal primary and secondary positions of power and opposition around a rectangular table. This arrangement is common in meetings of a committee of equals with an appointed chairman, or in meetings where the chairman has a higher position. The second table arrangement is likely when the meeting contains a hierarchy of personnel. I have noticed this pattern frequently in military meetings, where the general sits at the head of the table and those along the side

Committee

King Arthur Arrangement

Multiple King Arthurs

Key:

X = Dominant Positions
O = Secondary Dominant Positions
➜ = Direction of Decreasing Status

Figure 2–4. Table status.

are arranged by rank, with the lowly lieutenants sitting meekly at the far end. This is sometimes called the King Arthur arrangement, in honor of the round table, which supposedly had no status. (Instead, the knights fought to see who could sit closest to King Arthur.) The third table in Figure 2–4 shows a multiple King Arthur arrangement where each executive has grouped his minions around him. In this situation, relative status is determined by the number of chairs between a person and his or her King Arthur. See if these observations about seating behavior hold in your organization. You may find that this is one of the primary indicators of power.

REAR FEAR

There is a special case of seating dynamics called rear fear, which may date back to the wild, wild West.

"Okay, you cowpokes and gunslingers. What's the one rule to follow when you're sipping your favorite firewater at the Longbranch? That's right, tenderfoot, never sit with your back to the door! You never know when some filthy varmint will come up and plug ya' in the back." Today, people will first fill the restaurant tables along the wall and may even leave rather than sit in the middle of the dining area.

People do not like to sit with their backs to the door because it makes them feel exposed. Less than one percent of the offices I have seen are arranged facing away from the door. One that was, the office of a principal in a CPA firm, caused people to sit down in the *occupant's* chair instead of the visitor's chair, which faced the door. Even though the layout of the office was clear, the visitor could not imagine that the principal would sit with his back exposed. Another office arranged "backward" had a beautiful view of St. Louis' Gateway Arch, which the advertising-executive occupant could not bear to miss.

Your relationship to the door is also important in meetings or negotiating sessions. If you wish to feel more secure, try to sit with your back to the wall. If you don't want to overpower others, let them sit facing the door. Sitting with your back to the door can be very disruptive, because frequent noises from outside may drive your curiosity to the breaking point. Some negotiators use a noise in the hall or interruptions such as a secretary coming in to ask, "Is George Finster here? There's been a terrible accident," to unsettle their opposites. There may not even be a George Finster, but everyone will go crazy wondering what the "accident" was. Start noticing what is behind you and others, be it a wall or a door, and try to determine how it is affecting your sense of security and comfort.

Zones of Attention

Where we sit can greatly affect our attentiveness at a meeting, presentation, or lecture. In college, I knew many students who forced themselves to sit in the front row because they knew they would learn more there. We have all been in the position of arriving late and having to go to the front of the room for the only available chairs, watched every step of the way by the audience and speaker! Once settled, there we sat, uncomfortably exposed to the probing eyes of the lecturer. Afraid to show our attention lagging, we hung on every word, no matter how dull.

People in this "front and center" position give the most attention to the speaker. Those in the middle section pay the next highest amount of attention and ask questions next most frequently. The middle zone is a good, safe area, with people comfortably surrounded by others. Attention and interaction decrease as the listener sits farther back in the room. The side zones are even less responsive and attentive.

The worst listening area is filled with "balcony Baptists." I once had an elderly neighbor who would sit in the balcony of the local church and sleep. It was a very considerate sleep, though, since he learned to hold his head at an angle that would reflect the chandeliers' light from his glasses into the pulpit. That way, he felt he wasn't insulting the pastor by blatantly sleeping through the sermons. In any meeting room, remember: "If you want to see them sleep, sit them deep!"

It's better to arrange the seats a little deeper than wider, after going beyond the first few rows. Try to keep a depth-to-width ratio of about 3 to 2 before lengthening the rows. This way, you will keep more people involved. Also, don't ignore the territorial space needs of your audience. It's better to have 80 percent of the crowd present, comfortable, and attentive than to have 100 percent of your audience crowded and unruly. (The missing 20 percent will be told you were wonderful anyway, which is better than hearing you and leaving it to chance.)

If you can set up a lecture room, keep the door to your side or back. That way, if there is an interruption, you can control it, resolve it in front of your listeners so they can satisfy their curiosity, and continue without waiting for people to turn around again and settle in their seats. If you are plagued with latecomers, such as at an after-dinner speech or early morning meeting, arrange the chairs with the door in the rear and leave four or five chairless rows in the back as a noise buffer zone. Don't overstock the room with chairs before your audience arrives. People will sit as far back as you let them. Set up a few chairs in the buffer zone at the beginning of the meeting; otherwise you'll have half the audience sitting back there from the start.

If you are attending a meeting, find out who else will be there ahead of time. Arrive early enough (without being the first) to have your choice of seats if possible. Let others have their backs to the door if it suits your purpose. Sit there yourself only when you *choose* to. Find out if you are part of a King Arthur competitive group. Sit close to your king if you can, but not too close to the head of the meeting, unless he or she is also your king. If you're one of the kings, determine ahead of time who is in control and what your attitude is toward the leader. Then choose your position accordingly. If you are the leader, you should be picking out your Stars and Heels, like Joe B. did in Chapter 1.

Finally, note the relative positions of the group. Who can you talk to easily and comfortably with no one else in the way? Who "opposes" you across the table? If the meeting has no formal leader, who has picked the leader's position nonverbally? If you wish to gain control, are you in the proper position for it? If you ask yourself these questions each time you sit down at a meeting, you will be well on your way to using seating dynamics successfully.

Office Etiquette

The moment enclosed offices are established in any organization, an unwritten procedure develops for entering an office and responding to a visitor. As a salesman, I enjoyed sitting in a reception area and watching the private offices while I waited for a customer. The relative status of the office occupant and the visitor was apparent the moment the visitor stepped up to the door.

For example, someone comes up to an office door, hesitates with a single brief knock, then proceeds in. The occupant looks up and waves the visitor to a chair. Who has the higher status? The visitor is most likely of a slightly lower status or an immediate underling who has a casual relationship with the superior. The two key points in this scene are the pause at the door and the boss's recognition of the subordinate.

If your home is your castle, then your office is your fortress. In general, a subordinate respects this and will pause at the door before entering. In the case above, the pause was almost negligible, connoting a close relationship or status. The longer the visitor waits at the door, the lower the status. If there is *no* wait—if the visitor strides in without pause—then the visitor has a *higher* status, showing no respect for a subordinate's office. The response of the office occupant is another indicator of relationships. The faster the occupant stands up, the higher the status of the visitor. In the case above, the occupant didn't stand up, but merely waved the subordinate to a chair. Had it been one of the organization's higher-level executives, the manager would have jumped from the chair!

NONPEOPLE

There is a small category of people who can break office etiquette without fear. A secretary can walk in and out of the boss's office without knocking. So can the maintenance personnel. The reason is that they are *nonpeople*, people having no status. In my seminars on professional development for women, only about 10 percent of the secretaries say that their boss introduces them by name (rather than as "my secretary") in a meeting. A maintenance man can enter a meeting room to replace a light bulb and the meeting will go on without a pause, as if he weren't there. Waiters and waitresses fall into this same category.

The invisibility of waiters is illustrated by a famous Groucho

Marx story. Groucho usually went to Chasen's for dinner after his *You Bet Your Life* show. One evening, some people were celebrating a birthday in an alcove right behind Groucho's booth. When waiters wheeled in a cake, Groucho got up, waved them away, and proceeded to cut the cake himself. He served the cake totally unnoticed by anyone in the alcove, came back to his table, and sat down.

"Hello. I'm Ken, and I'll be your waiter for this evening."

"Hello!" you respond, never bothering to introduce yourself. If people introduced themselves to you on the street, would you return the favor? Possibly. You certainly would in a business environment. The next time you are in a restaurant, introduce yourself back to the waiter or waitress and see what happens. You will have made a "person" out of both yourself and the employee serving you. In the business world, someone you convert from a nonperson to a person will pay back your thoughtfulness tenfold.

Treat your office with respect. One of my former bosses had a curious practice that stripped him of all office status. He kept a jar of candy sitting on a table by the door for anyone to take. People popped in and out, no matter what was going on, mumbling, "Just wanted this," "Thanks," or "Excuse me." Everyone had an excuse to enter his office at will, and people did, disrupting anyone else who was in there with him. He gained no status from his office. As a result, he had to close the door frequently, turning away legitimate visitors. He could have stopped the distractions more effectively (and saved some money) by killing the candy dish!

Start noticing your behavior when you enter any office in your organization. Do you uphold "office etiquette"? Are there subordinates who don't recognize yours? If you are vying for promotion with one of your contemporaries, who has a more casual relationship with your boss? Whom does your boss respect more? If you visit other offices as a consultant, auditor, or internal adviser, can you determine the relative status of people before you meet them and learn their names? These are all questions office etiquette can help answer.

Summary

This chapter illustrated the checklist for observing, analyzing, and controlling body location. The checklist shows you how to begin observing NVC by asking the questions:

1. What are the interaction distances? (TERRITORIAL SPACE)

2. What are the height relationships? (HEIGHT MIGHT)

3. Who is leading the group? (TREAD SPREAD)

4. Who has the psychological advantage of physical size? (SIZE PRIZE)

5. Where is everyone sitting and why? (SEATING DYNAMICS)

6. What respect is shown at the office? (OFFICE ETIQUETTE)

With practice, you will begin to ask these questions automatically, taking only a few moments to accurately size up a new situation. Start finding out how these nonverbal signals apply to your organization. It may seem as if you are looking at your company for the first time, seeing a whole new level of communication. You are, because you are now learning the vocabulary of NVC.

3

Indicators

So far, you have learned to observe and analyze where people put their bodies and why. The second NVC scan involves noting information about people's appearance and environment, including their possessions and ornaments. These points of observation are called *indicators*.

Duration of Indicators

Indicators vary in how long they remain consistent. The first time you meet someone, you will notice a number of pieces of information that you will not need to notice again because they will remain unchanged in later communications sessions. Other indicators will be consistent for only a single communications session. (Remember nonrepeatability from Chapter 1.) Still other indicators will not be consistent through even a single communications session.

It is important to separate the indicators you see by their consistency. If you assume a man will always have a mustache and use it to remember his name, you may be in trouble when he shaves it off. A woman student wore a different colored wig and a drastically different outfit the second day of one of my memory classes. Nearly two-thirds of the class had no idea who she was!

ENDURING INDICATORS

Enduring indicators do not change from communications session to communications session. Examples are physical items such as buildings, monuments, and terrain and personal items such as uniforms. Sometimes, these are more important than the people themselves.

Have you ever been in a hardware store in a suit or dress and had someone come up to you and ask about the location of an item? After you stop and explain that you are shopping too, the customer walks off glancing over his shoulder with a look that says, "Well, what were you standing there looking like a clerk for?"

Many stores have gone to the trouble and expense to outfit their salespeople in order to avoid the confusion. One local hardware chain made a big advertising campaign of having "orange-coated experts" in each of its departments. Their experts were the same old clerks in easily identifiable orange hunter's coats.

A police uniform confers automatic authority on the wearer. At one "enlightened" university, school officials abandoned the campus patrolman uniforms and the seldom-used weapons in favor of stylish blazer outfits. Within a few weeks almost the entire force resigned. The men felt that the blazers made their job harder. They stood out less in a crowd and had less control in a conflict situation. Supervisors felt that the uniforms had given the men automatic power and focused crowd attention on them, forcing the officers to act. The school quickly returned to the standard police-style uniform.

Consider the "nonperson" waitress from the last chapter. We often forget which waitress is ours because her uniform helps make her a nonperson, just as the maintenance man's getup makes him a nonperson to office workers. I've decided the best way to commit a crime unrecognized is to wear a McDonald's hamburger clerk shirt and pants and sing, "We do it all for you!" Guaranteed, witnesses will see only what I wear and not who I am. Unusual physical features, such as facial scars, can have the same attention-focusing effect. "What color was the hair, officer?" "Gee, I don't know. But he did have this horrible scar!"

Physical characteristics may or may not be enduring. The McDonald's disguise and scar are not going to last long after the crime. Hair color, hairstyle, weight, and even facial features may change. John Barrymore's profile was enduring for him, but Phyllis Diller's face endured only until her lift. So make certain to sort out what you are likely to see again.

Be alert for a change in the norm. Many a husband has come home and wished that he had noticed that new dress or hairstyle. Don't take anything for granted, in your personal life or in business. One afternoon, I was calling on a regular customer and waited briefly while he handled a phone call. I noticed a new painting on a wall I had seen at least 200 times. This made me curious, so I began to scan the room for anything else out of the ordinary. As I glanced over the large bookcase beside his desk, I noticed a binder with a competitor's name on it, a binder that I had not seen before. It turned out that the customer's entire staff had been to a competitive demonstration covering something I had recently proposed. I questioned the customer carefully about the binder's contents and began to compete for my sale. I may have won the order even if I hadn't seen the binder, but my position would not have been as strong.

TEMPORARY INDICATORS

Indicators can also be temporary, lasting only one communications session. Clothing, hairstyle, weather, health, time of day, and location are usually not consistent from session to session. Weather has a tremendous effect on our behavior. Grade school teachers know well that they are in for a long day when there is a steady rain. People who wouldn't even glance in sympathy at a car in a ditch will be out there helping a motorist in a snowstorm.

Some people prefer hot weather and some prefer cold. A friend of mine is a cold-weather person, can't stand the heat. Put her in a hot room and she will agree to anything to get out. I would much rather be too warm than too cold. I once taught a four-hour college class in a room adjacent to a boiler. While the rest of the building was down to an energy-conserving 68 degrees (to which everyone was accustomed), our room was in the high 70s. Even though I was on my feet lecturing for four hours, I felt fine after class. The students, however, came out looking like they had spent an afternoon inside a punching bag. So always take into account the weather environment of your session.

Time of day is another important part of people's environment. Some of us are evening people and some are day people. I wake up groggy and don't get going until late morning. I have another period in the day, about 4:00 to 6:00 P.M., that I call my "dead spot," when I am again sluggish. I pick up right after dinner and can go full speed until I drop into bed. For example, I wrote most of this book after 7:00 P.M. Anyone wanting to sell me something or get my commitment for action would have a tough time during my dead periods. My wife and family know this and are careful to approach me at my best times of day.

Others are day people. These are the bright, eager-to-work, bushy-tailed folks we early groaners hate. Day people usually close up shop early and use the evening hours for relaxation or light work. I had a sales partner who was like this. As the workload increased, he would get to work earlier and earlier, and want me to be there too. I tried it for a short time but succeeded only in destroying my entire cycle for several days. I contemplated murdering him, figuring I could claim justifiable homicide, but I was afraid I would get a "morning" judge.

Certain times of day are bad for *all* people. How do you feel when you sit in a meeting, class, or seminar after lunch? Doesn't it seem like the world is moving in slow motion? Nothing is more miserable than wanting to fall asleep and knowing you can't. I have spent many a class fighting this feeling for two hours every day. The main reason we get sleepy after lunch is that our stomach is robbing our brain of blood.

Be aware of the time factor in your communications sessions. I know whether all the important people I deal with are night or day people and in what environment they feel most comfortable. If you don't know, ask them. Maybe you have asked the boss for a raise at the wrong time of the day, or when he is uncomfortable or irritable. An eager young management trainee I knew could hardly wait for her boss to get in to begin her appraisal. What she didn't know was that his car air conditioner had failed that morning and he showed up for work blazing in more ways than one. Had she postponed the meeting until another day, or at least until he had cooled off, she would have fared much better. Had *he* been sensitive, he would have postponed it. Don't make either mistake by ignoring the time of day and the environment.

Start noticing how healthy the other person feels. None of us are effective when we don't feel well. Sales have been lost or raises delayed because the customer or boss had a bad cold. A more insidious form of "bad health" is having to go to the bathroom. What may come across as impatience may actually be acute pain in trying to avoid the embarrassment of leaving to go to the bathroom. Many women find it particularly difficult to say, "Excuse me, I have to go to the john," grab their purse, and leave. Men are less likely to have this problem, although some may find it awkward. An executive I know used this bathroom embarrassment as a domination factor. He always had lunch brought up during long, intensive planning sessions so his people had to disrupt the meeting to go to the bathroom. He felt his personal discomfort in "holding it" was worth it to ensure faster acceptance of his ideas, the most important of which he saved until last.

Be aware of the one-time conditions that exist throughout a communications session. Watch and compare what stays constant and what changes. We are influenced by a host of environmental and physical factors, any one of which can have a drastic effect on the messages we send and receive in any given situation. These factors are another reason why communication is not repeatable.

MOMENTARY INDICATORS

Indicators can also be momentary, lasting only part of the communications session. Examples are distractions, changing locale, visual aids, and even doodles. These momentary items or events can drastically change the course of a session for the better or the worse.

Distractions are the most frequent occurrence. The manager

who kept the candy dish in his office was so plagued by distractions that he spent most of his day with the door closed. This only increased the candy traffic when the door was open, which led to more door-closed time, and so on. Because of these constant interruptions, his people either avoided talking to him during the day or sought him out before and after regular working hours when they would have a better chance of seeing him without interruption.

The phone is another common distraction. America has a cultural phone-answering compulsion, undoubtedly fostered from the start by Alexander Graham himself. He was no dummy when he designed the device with a ring mechanism. (As comedian George Carlin points out, "Isn't it nice that the phone wasn't designed by Alexander Graham Siren?") The baby may be screaming, the sink overflowing, the office on fire, but we'll still answer that incessantly ringing little monster.

All executive training should include a session in *not* answering the phone. Many an important meeting has been wasted by a "short" 20-minute phone call. With one of my managers, who was addicted to phone answering, I would walk out of the room on any phone call lasting more than five minutes. I always explained leaving with, "Oh, I saw that you were going to be busy and I didn't want to seem like I was listening in. Besides, I had other things to do until you were free." This attitude has several advantages. First, you aren't reminded of your lowly status by sitting around wasting your time while your boss is handling "more important" work. Second, you are gently urging your boss to stop the practice because you won't "sit still" for it. Finally, you may get a phone call in the meantime that will make the boss wait on you.

There is one effective way to handle a distraction when you are speaking. I was giving a sales presentation training seminar for a group from a large firm. About a half-hour into my talk, a shapely young woman came in and filled in the sole remaining chair. My audience was gone the minute she opened the door. Realizing that the group was thinking about techniques, but not "speaking" techniques, I shut up. The group finally noticed that I had not been talking about three or four seconds after she sat down. Not wanting to miss the opportunity, I asked them, "What do you do during a distraction?'' To a man (and woman) they answered, "Nothing!" If your audience, be it one person or many, is distracted, stop and let yourself be distracted too. When it's over with, the attention will return and your audience will be ready to continue. Like most powerful emotions, curiosity is short-lived. Let it be satisfied before you get back to work.

Beware of changing locale during a session. A young man planned a luncheon date with his boss to discuss his performance and the possibility of a raise. He wisely chose a restaurant where they could talk discreetly, but he made a fatal error in timing. Walking over to the place, his boss innocently asked about the subject of their lunch, and rather than deferring the young man began his prepared talk. You can imagine the results after dropping off their coats, waiting at the receptionist's table, ordering lunch with frequent visits from the waiter (drink order, drinks, lunch order, lunch, and those ever present water and coffee fillers), and chomping on their meals. The program was never allowed to unfold.

Fortunately, in this instance the manager wasn't negative, but the young man accomplished nothing and missed a chance to further himself. The interference of changing location and then eating was too much for the conversation. The ideal time for the conversation would have been *after* lunch. They both would have been relaxed and the manager softened up.

As a rule, don't change locations. If you have to move, always move to a *better* location for communication. A good example is eating dinner then going to a different room for a presentation, or getting someone out of personal territory into a neutral area or into your territory. The best approach is to control the timing of your communications so that the location can become a temporary environment rather than a momentary one.

Any group of visuals, whether formal aids or extemporaneous doodles, are momentary indicators. There is a wealth of NVC material in visuals. A useful trick in meetings is to be the last one to leave so that you can look at the doodles on all the remaining pads. If it is your meeting, make sure there are pads to use and that you leave last. If you are merely an attendee and can't leave last, make sure to take all your papers with you so you don't provide any unplanned information.

Employees of a radio station in Florida were caught by police going through a rival station's trash. Station personnel had managed to piece together an entire promotional campaign from meeting notes taken during planning sessions. Because of the bad publicity generated by the arrest, the station was forced to return the material, but it still gained a marketing coup. Don't let one of *your* rivals do the same.

A visual aid is a special, controlled type of distraction. It takes attention away from you, so you must return the favor to be effective. I once saw visuals so concise that a monkey would have looked knowledgeable using them. The audience realized it and gave due credit to the presenter who developed them. I have also seen visuals that looked as if they had been drawn by a monkey. The audience was equally unimpressed with the speaker using them. Remember that visuals should be used only when words and body alone are not as effective; they are a distraction with a purpose. Make sure you are presenting your visuals instead of vice versa.

Identifying indicators is really an exercise in increasing your skills of observation. Once you are familiar with the important indicators of the people you deal with, you can sort the indicators by their consistency. Some will be constant throughout your acquaintance with the person, some will last only during a session, and a few will vary from moment to moment.

The indicator checklist is divided into three parts:

Personal
Shared
Public

As the names imply, these indicators vary with respect to how large a group they provide information about. Personal indicators apply to individuals; shared indicators apply to a group such as a company or a club; and public indicators apply to a large group, usually related geographically.

Personal Indicators

If there is one common trait exhibited by humanity, it is the overwhelming drive to decorate its nest. I have not been in a single office that was not in some way customized by its occupant. Even in sparsely decorated offices, some form of humanizing has taken place.

POSSESSIONS AND DECOR

My sales office was a good example of the way people personalize their surroundings. All the desks were out in the middle of big, open rooms, set side by side with only two-drawer file cabinets separating them. Each desk was equipped with a phone. (This unappealing environment may have been intentional—to keep the salesmen out of the office—but I suspect that it was also inexpensive.) Despite the antiseptic atmosphere, each desk was in some way personalized. Managers had small name plates posted on the front of their desks, but the names weren't really needed. The belongings and paraphernalia on each desk were enough to immediately identify whose desk it was.

There were bookends with an abundance of work-related books; there were trophies and awards from contests and classes; and there were those miscellaneous little items that are the most revealing. My desk had a chunk of artificial turf with a little Miami Dolphins helmet on it to ward off the St. Louis Cardinal fans. I also had a Ziggy cartoon saying, "Today is a whole new day to screw up in," in honor of my usual status with management. Another cartoon, a reminder of my first commission check, featured Seminole Sam of Pogo protesting that he at one time amassed a fortune of $24.60 in due bills.

Other desks had such things as a soldered-nail basketball player, a plastic Charlie the Tuna radio, plants, United Van Lines toy trucks, mistake erasers, family picture cubes, a toy mailbox, and a boat on a bendable wire. Many items were even useful. I had an artificial turf telephone pad so my phone would sound different from the 20 or so adjacent phones. There was a myriad of phone number holders, appointment books, and phone note holders. Each desk was truly a reflection of its owner. Even the trash around the desk was indicative of the person who used it. Look around your office and you will probably come up with a list of items as wacky as the one above.

Even though the salespeople in my office spent only a small portion of their time at their desks, a great deal of personalizing was still in evidence. There was even more individualization in the managerial offices. In addition to desk paraphernalia, almost every wall and piece of furniture had some personal touch. Paintings and pictures were in abundance. Managers were sure to include anything of status in their gallery of framed pictures. Boat pictures are good, if the boat is big. A picture of the office occupant standing beside his or her airplane is even better. The most impressive personal picture of this type belonged to the chief of pilots of a small airline. The picture showed him standing on the con of a nuclear sub—a duty he had pulled during his reserve summer tour. How many people do you know who have been aboard a nuclear sub *on duty?*

Paintings are also a good source of information about the occupant's tastes. At the very least, they are conversation pieces. Be careful, though, in making comments about a painting or work of art: you can offend even if you intend to compliment. I once stuck my foot in my mouth with incredible grace and speed by trying to be nice. I complimented an executive on a painting he had displayed, only to find out that he had just moved into the office and hated the painting but hadn't had time to do anything about it. Paintings often grow old or stale to the person living in the office. The best thing to do if you want to talk about a painting is to ask a question about it rather than offering a blind comment.

Degrees, certificates, and awards are other effective wall decorations. They will tell you what the occupant's activities are and what he or she is proud of. They usually come in the standard $8^{1}/_{2}'' \times 11''$ size and are displayed in clusters. If you wish to display some of these in your office, make certain they create a positive effect. For example, when I left my sales position, I had two plaques and certificates of achievement for making my company's 100 percent quota club. When I left my island desk to set up my own office, I decided to decorate my work area with some of these items. When I put my four items on the wall, they looked naked, almost obscene. I had seen managers with a string of them running from floor to ceiling in their offices. My little display was somewhat underwhelming.

Decorations can be overdone too. I visited a business consultant who had approximately 25 framed documents on his office wall. When I noncommitally mentioned them, he apologized for the number, telling me that there were four more being framed! This display might have been awe inspiring, except that he had obviously mounted every document he had ever received. There were fraternal awards of the kind that are passed out like pancakes (an Optimist Club executive calls them "M&Ms for the troops"). There were also letters of appreciation, certificates of membership, and one or two outstanding meeting awards. The net effect was to appear ostentatious.

I believe the properly impressive number of framed business items is five to eight. The typical mixture might include two Degrees from Somewhere, a couple of Certified Professional Somethings, and a Member of the Year Award from the Affiliated Associates Association. Make sure they are in the same style of frame so that their number, rather than content, is what strikes the visitor.

Unique or bizarre decorations are also status grabbers. Imagine the company president asking you about the African witchdoctor's mask hanging on your wall. How can he top you when you answer, "Oh, I picked that little thing up on my last trip to the continent"? You know all he's had time for is the stockholders' meeting in Attumswa, Iowa.

Items that are totally unfathomable have the same effect. Prominently display some unimaginable object at the front of your desk. Natural curiosity will force your visitors to ask what it is, in which case you are one up on them. If they don't ask about it, idly play with it as you talk. You will at least distract them, giving yourself a further advantage. A hot item with the computer folks was a printer counterweight, a heavy cylindrical piece of metal that slid in and out of a plastic sleeve. It had no reasonable purpose, but its moving parts gave it a high fondle value.

Puzzles are also good for maintaining control over your callers. I had one customer who kept a small block puzzle on his desk for this very purpose. I studiously ignored it, being careful not to even look at it lest that allow my customer to bring it up. One day he caught me when we started talking about a mutual hobby, puzzles. He suddenly told me, "Well, if you like puzzles, why don't you try this one?" and shoved the block at me. Then he held up his arm and started looking at his watch, saying, "I just want to see how long it takes you; don't mind me."

As all of us who have stood before a group in silence know, a minute can be interminable. I managed to get the block assembled after two and a half minutes, which rated, "That's not too bad, Ken." Before I was buried in any more condescending remarks, I cut the meeting short and beat a hasty retreat. Before the next call on this customer, I memorized a set of ten pencil-and-paper logic puzzles. I resolved that if stumped again, I would at least be able to *trade* puzzles. So beware of any desk puzzles you see. They can be used to inflict major psychological damage.

APPEARANCE

We all place a tremendous amount of importance on physical appearance. Not only does it provide basic demographic data on age, sex, height, weight, race, and physical beauty. It also provides a wealth of data on personality. Appearance is so important to us that we have a special term for our initial analysis of it, the first impression.

First Impressions

A first impression is the "love at first sight" of the business world. We know the importance of making a good first impression, since we "never have a second chance to make a good first impression." Yet so few of us know what first impression we give. I use a first-impression fact-finding procedure in my communications classes. As each person introduces himself or herself at the beginning of the class, the students write on a note card five traits they think best describe this person. When the introductions are completed, the cards are distributed to the attendees. They then have a data base of first-impression traits from their peers, given anonymously. Frequently, the cards are quite similar in content and provide a good composite of the first impression the student creates. Grouping similar adjectives, such as intelligent/smart/quick or ambitious/aggressive/go-getter, gives an even better composite picture.

A refinement in this first-impression procedure is to have class members write down what caused them to list a certain trait for a student. This gives the student valuable feedback. For example, a middle-aged female supervisor had a tendency to wear "girlish clothes"—short skirts and puffy-sleeved blouses long out of style. Her image was one of a child skipping home from school. This revelation prompted her to make an immediate wardrobe change, using one of the other female executives for guidance.

Clothing has an enormous effect on the first impression you project. John T. Molloy has analyzed the effect of various types of men's and women's clothing in his books on "wardrobe engineering." Almost all his research methods were based on first impressions. He showed different clothing styles to individuals and then asked them to draw conclusions about the people wearing the clothes. Molloy's *Dress for Success* and *The Woman's Dress for Success Book* offer valuable information on clothing styles in business.

It is well worth your time to find out the first impression you send out. If you don't have an opportunity to use the classroom method of introduction ask one of your close friends to give you a candid assessment. Or have a friend find out for you by informally questioning your associates. Try to tie the impressions back to specific characteristics or traits, and don't be defensive!

Body Styles

You can also benefit by appraising your physical characteristics for data on your appearance. One of the primary appearance factors is body style. This doesn't include hardtop, convertible, or hatchback, but hefty, muscular, or slender.

The Hefty is the round, fat person. He or she is considered to be good-natured and jolly, with an untiring sense of humor. Typical Hefties are Santa Claus or Curley (of the Three Stooges). Hefties have a number of unpleasant image characteristics to fight. They are thought to have overindulged themselves (even when their problem is medical). The thinner members of society think, "Too bad the poor thing doesn't have the willpower to stop eating."

Overweight people often have a difficult time looking neat. Today's styles were not made for the large person to wear comfortably. The ideal style for a Hefty is probably a toga affair draped over the body instead of the close-fitting, complicated clothes that have been in fashion for hundreds of years. On Hefties, shirts or blouses pull out at the waist, pants or slacks ride up as people sit down, and all the constrictions around the neck, arms, and legs accentuate the loose skin. Other areas of the outfit have to be baggy in order to provide enough give without ripping when sitting or turning. It is extremely difficult to look sharp.

There are ways to minimize this problem. People do not have to be fashion designers or coordinators to choose styles that overcome the negatives of too much size. They may have to pay a little more for clothes, but it can be well worth it to have outfits individually tailored for the best possible fit.

A varying weight makes it harder to look neat consistently, though. If weight fluctuates too much, the clothes have to be big enough for the upward swing and will look baggy the rest of the time. One executive on a massive weight reduction program suffered through this process. His clothes were always too big. Since he couldn't afford a new suit every 15 pounds, he had his suits cut down. When he finally reached his target weight, he rewarded himself with a completely new wardrobe and threw out all his old clothes in celebration. The entire office was aware of his weight loss, and the executive actually gained status from the baggy suits, which became a symbol of his willpower and determination. (He also became the best-dressed man in the office.)

Another way to avoid the sloppy look is to primp often. An oversized salesman made a habit of stopping by the men's room in any office building where he was going to make a call. He would straighten himself out after the car ride and then proceed. He made the point that taking this time was important to his image. He never walked into an office with his hair blown, tie crooked, collar up, or shoes muddy. You shouldn't either.

The second body type is the Muscular. These are the people with athletic builds, the kind that adorn our daytime serials and fill up Muscle Beach. When I was in college, there was a standing joke about guys who went out for track, which was my sport. When all the athletes came in to take showers in the afternoon after their workouts, you could tell each one's sport by his behavior. The football players would come in, bend the showerhead pipe to the proper angle, soap themselves up and begin throwing soap at everybody. The basketballers would come in and loop their towels over the water pipes near the ceiling. The wrestlers would come in looking like little Mr. Americas, wishing they could drink the water instead of wash in it. The baseballers would amble in, every pore of their bodies oozing coordination. The skinny, scrawny guys who didn't look like any sort of athletes were trackmen.

The problem for trackmen was that everyone else in the shower, even most of the basketball players, were those disgusting Musculars. They were the ones who best filled out their letter jackets, had coeds hanging off each arm, and had muscles where trackmen didn't even have places.

Don't underestimate the advantage that a Muscular possesses in the world of NVC. In the 1976 presidential campaign, former President Ford proudly stated that he could still hike a football and fire off the line just as he did years ago at Michigan. And the public believed him. Unlike many Presidents, Ford skied, swam, and played golf. He left office as fit as or more fit than when he went in.

Musculars seem more self-reliant, more mature. Can you imagine 1976 Olympic decathlon champion Bruce Jenner begging his wife to let him go out and shoot pool with the guys? Can you picture John Wayne throwing a tantrum when something didn't go his way? Is Billie Jean King stuck at home because Larry won't let her out? Would Tarzan have been of any interest to us if he had looked like a trackman or the Goodyear blimp? Many top executives of major companies are Musculars—perhaps as high as 80 to 90 percent in some corporations. Do they fit this mold in your company? Do you?

If you do, don't destroy it. Put yourself on a diet to fight the mid-20s to mid-30s metabolism change that seems to catch so many people. Don't let an hour and half of eating jeopardize the eight hours per day of work you put into being successful. If you don't fit the mold, try to get there. There is a definite relationship between a sound body and business success. With growth of racquet sports, indoor sports facilities, health clubs, and adult athletic programs, you should be able to find *something* that interests you. Find it and let it develop into a habit!

The third body type is the Slender. Tall, thin, and fragile, Slenders are the kind of people who need ten pounds to look thin. Most Slenders can eat freely and heavily without the slightest weight change. This can be a curse, though, because under many an older Hefty resides a young Slender who couldn't modify his or her eating habits during the metabolism change. If you haven't yet faced this crisis, be prepared to act when that scale indicator begins to drift toward the right.

Being a Slender is not particularly better than being a Hefty, just different. Slenders appear to be tense and nervous. Their gestures are more accentuated because of their thinness, and they appear to be moving faster and less smoothly. Comedian Don Knotts developed this style to perfection in his "nervous" routine. It was a terrible shock to see him on a Steve Allen TV special talking normally.

There are several ways to dispel the slender image. Don't accentuate your thinness with clothing. Ignore form-fit blouse or shirt and pants styles. Stay away from vertically striped fabrics, which give Slenders a beanpole or picket fence look. Coats should be cut fuller (but not baggy). Vests can add bulk. Ties should be as wide as fashionably possible, without making you look like Corky the Clown. Avoid sleeveless sweaters or blouses, since they make your arms look like sticks coming out of a pipe.

Another step is to slow down. Gesture less rapidly, walk slower, and in general give the image of care and forethought. Make your gestures more muted. If you have a nervous habit such as nail biting, finger twisting, or cuticle picking, concentrate on eliminating it. With your body style, the habit will be magnified and reinforce the nervous stereotype.

Slenders too need regular exercise. There is a world of difference between fatless muscle and toned muscle. While few Slenders may be able to turn themselves into Musculars, they can benefit from the positive nonverbal signals that the "in shape" person transmits.

Whatever your body style, be aware of what your physical appearance transmits. Begin to think of body style as a changeable trait, not a permanent feature. If you don't like your current equipment, now is the time to start modifying it. If you don't want to put out the effort to change yourself, at least analyze what you are and minimize any negative effects through clothing and grooming. Give your body real "style" and you will have another NVC plus.

SHARED INDICATORS

Shared indicators include large, immovable, or difficult-to-move objects such as offices, desks, statues, and bookcases. Michael Korda, in his book *Power*, makes a detailed study of the relationships of office location and status. He points out that corner offices reflect the most power and status within an organization. The architect for the Community Federal Savings and Loan building in St. Louis incorporated this idea into the design. To make it a more attractive lease property in the highly competitive St. Louis office-space market, the architect provided more corner offices than the conventional square or rectangular structure. (See Figure 3–1.)

Office size and furnishings are also indicative of status. I have never seen a subordinate's office better furnished than a manager's office if the two are physically close to each other. Even if the subordinate has a larger office, the manager's office is usually better located.

Many companies have a carpeted "executive's row" with limited access through a screening secretary. Most managers would rather take a cut in salary than pass up a chance to join the row. One large utility went so far as to locate its top executives in a different building, a plush office in the downtown business area a mile or so from the main location. The corporate officers and the two executive vice-presidents were the only occupants of the facility and had almost half a floor of space. This was the ultimate in status. Even subordinates at the vice-presidential level had to get in their car, fight traffic, park, and make their way to the executive offices for any meeting. The top executives *never* went to the main office building. In addition, the main office building was constructed with metal walls and partitions. The nicest office in the building still looked like the inside of a refrigerator, while the executive suites had more wood in them than a lumber dealer.

Figure 3–1. Corner-office building.
(Courtesy Community Federal Savings and Loan Association, St. Louis, Missouri)

The working environment reinforced the status of the office occupants.

Desks are another status indicator. At the lower levels, size is the important feature. The bigger your desk, the greater your status. Ideally, I suppose, you should have a desk that looks like a roller rink. At the higher levels, size is often a minor factor, with simplicity taking precedence. As noted earlier, some chief executives are doing away with the business desk and installing ornate tables of the same size. This is similar to the executive who doesn't wear a watch, which says in effect, "I don't have to worry about what time it is. My assistants will keep me informed, or everyone else will have to conform to my schedule regardless of the time." A drawerless table says much the same thing. "I don't have to store materials for retrieval, nor do I do the type of work that requires me to dig into papers all over my desk." This executive will keep a simple office with a clean desk at all times.

Books are another shared indicator that provides a great deal of information about the owner. I recently met with the chairman of a management program in a local university. As I walked in, I noticed massive bookshelves lining one wall. We were interrupted briefly by the phone after I sat down, so I spent the time looking at the titles on the shelf. I was surprised that the chairman of a management program would have so many finance-oriented books. When our conversation resumed, I opened with, "How did you manage to switch from a finance professorship to chair a management department?" He began to answer and suddenly stopped, asking, "How did you know that?" I explained about the evidence on the shelves, and he gave me one of Dr. Watson's frequent comments to Sherlock Holmes, "Oh, that's obvious. Why didn't I think of it?"

Bookshelf ogling is easy and is an excellent way to learn the tastes and interests of the owner of the books. It is also a good way to build rapport with a new acquaintance during those first awkward minutes. One small warning, though. Don't be tempted to load up *your* shelves with impressive titles you have never read. If you are asked about one of the books you've never opened, you expose yourself as a fake. So choose books you have read or at least know about, selecting the books to represent the image you wish to project. If you are a young college grad trying to project maturity and good judgment, stick to business-oriented books from well-known authors. If you want to project intelligence, go heavy on psychology and esoterica with big-worded titles that no one has ever heard of. Quoting from these books will also help maintain your image.

One manager I encountered decided to go with the "intelligence" image. He loaded his office with classical paintings, "heavy" books, strange desk puzzles, and obscure sayings. He was indeed intelligent and emphasized the point well. Eventually he was promoted to a job in a development division where intelligence and creativity were requirements for success. He used his personal and shared indicators to help create the image necessary for his promotion.

Public Indicators

Public indicators are the things around us that are not only shared but also open to the general public. Examples are houses, museums, monuments, shopping centers, highways, buildings, stadiums, and parks. These are indicative of our culture and of our living habits. Certain public artifacts are also good measures of social status and can communicate a great deal about an individual.

For example, where we live is important. A successful executive had very strong ideas about buying a house. He felt he should buy one that he would be better able to afford in three years. The house should be the lowest-priced house in a high-priced neighborhood and big enough so that he would not have to move out unless he was transferred (in which case the company would pay). The house he bought has doubled in value and is worth approximately 75 percent as much as the average house in his area. More important, he lives in *the* neighborhood in his city, one whose average house costs far more than what people at his job level normally pay.

This is a great advantage. The small corporation he works for hired a new president from the outside, over the current line of executives. The new president, unfamiliar with the area and buying within his salary, bought a suitable house in the city. He later found out that our executive had a better house and was located in a more exclusive area. Now the executive loves to entertain his boss and associates in his home whenever possible.

I once interviewed for a position at a manufacturing plant nestled in a mountain valley 70 miles from the nearest city with a population over 50,000. The entire social life of the area centered around the plant activities and a country club with a nine-hole golf course. Membership in the club was restricted (informally, of course) to executives and managers from the plant. I was truly impressed when I was offered a membership if I went to work at the plant, since this was the highest status I could hope to attain in the area. Fortunately for me (as my wife said at the time), I wanted something more than a life centered around work and a nine-hole golf course.

Just as certain areas of a city have more status than others, so some cities are considered more prestigious than others. Anyone born and living outside of New York has felt the patronizing attitude of those inhabitants of the nation's largest city. New York becomes a source of "war stories" for outsiders. Mastering its customs is a rite of passage for the newcomer. A friend of mine who moved there from a Midwestern city was driving like a madman within a year. He would trample crippled beggars without breaking stride and had a wealth of "New York stories" to pass on to us country bumpkins. As proof of the status he'd gained, he would be asked on his trips back to the Midwest, "What's it like up there?"

Other areas are also touted for their prestige. Texas has its cowboy driving a Cadillac with longhorns on the hood, California has its free and easy "space captain," and Florida has its retirees. For varied reasons, people in each of these areas can justifiably look down on others, gaining status in the process.

Summary

Chapter 2 presented the first NVC checklist for observing and controlling where people put their bodies and why. This chapter introduced the checklist for interpreting people's appearance and what they put around them. In analyzing yourself and others for these nonverbal indicators, try to answer the following questions:

1. What are people's possessions and appearance characteristics? (PERSONAL INDICATORS)

2. What items do people have in common? (SHARED INDICATORS)

3. What categories or groups do people fit into? (PUBLIC INDICATORS)

The key to success with all indicators is observation. Take every opportunity to observe the objects around the people you communicate with. Look at the desk, the furniture, the office. Find out where a person lives and why. The more you understand about how a person decorates the nest and why it is located where it is, the better you will understand the person.

The third NVC checklist, in the following chapter, will help you interpret what people do with their bodies once they have settled into a location.

4

Body Movements

The study of body motions, called *kinesics* (from the Greek word for movement), is a relatively new science. Begun in the early 1950s by a researcher with the unlikely name of Birdwhistell and popularized by Julius Fast in his book *Body Language,* kinesics has had little application to the business world. Until now its principles have not been organized into an easy-to-apply method for people in business. Such a method is now available with the five-point body scan:

> Center
> Head
> Posture
> Hands
> Legs

This scan will help you to "hear better with your glasses on." The body scan lets you observe others in an organized "head to toe" fashion.

Although interpretations will be given for various NVC signals, it's important to keep in mind that *each item in the scan must be checked before any conclusions can be drawn.* As the example from Chapter 1 with the customer who covered his mouth showed, movements are not traits. Readable movements must come in clusters, because no one sign in and of itself is indicative of anything (except the sign reader's gullibility). But this is not a particularly severe limitation. Most situations include enough movement indicators to allow you to draw at least broad conclusions—unless people are purposely trying to withhold their feelings. Even that is a nonverbal signal, usually followed by the question "Is there something wrong?"

Center

Imagine a rod going through the middle of your chest to the middle of your shoulder blades. (My wife has wished this were true several times.) Then imagine another rod from armpit to armpit ("underarm" just doesn't seem to have the same impact as "armpit"). Where these imaginary rods connect in your chest is your "center," as shown in Figure 4–1. The center is perhaps the most reliable and important body indicator. It is the only sign that can ever be successfully taken out of context and is a key indicator of how we feel about ourselves and others around us.

The center can be open, closed, aggressive, or submissive. We achieve an open center by standing erect and facing the person we are communicating with. We close our center by buttoning our coat or blazer, slumping, crossing our arms in umpire fashion, sitting with a chair back facing forward, or turning away from the person to talk over our shoulder. Our center becomes

Figure 4–1. The center.

aggressive with our chest out, shoulders back, and chin out, much like a Marine sergeant hazing his "boots." Our center becomes submissive when it is "buried" with bent posture, bowed shoulders, and a downcast gaze.

Occasionally, I'll begin a lecture by walking in front of the group slumped over, picking at my cuticles, and offering in a halting voice, "W-w-well, I'm the communicator. I'm here to teach you how to be effective like I am." You can hear a groan go through the audience as they glance around to spot the doors best suited for an inconspicuous exit. Or I may walk in with body erect, coat buttoned, and arms stiffly held at the sides, announcing loudly, "Hello, I'm Ken Cooper. I am your friend because—I care. You can tell me your problems in complete confidence and know I will help." With this introduction, I can see lips and tongues being bitten all over the room with the thought, "Oh, no, what have I gotten myself into?"

Other times I stride out with coat open, chest thrust out, arms clasped behind my back, and firmly state, "I'm Ken Cooper. You're going to like this class because you need this class. We will have one ten-minute break in the morning and one in the afternoon and that is all because we have a lot to do. Are there any questions?" There never are, of course, because they are too busy trying to see if I am armed.

After each of these shocks, I revert to my normal likable self and begin talking about what my approach made them think about me and the coming talk. My movements, of course, involved more than manipulating my center, but most students later agree that the center is a key indicator. In general, an open center indicates a friendly, positive attitude toward a person. A closed center is negative. Shake hands with someone face to face, and then shake hands with your shoulders pointing at the person looking over your right shoulder. See how less friendly the second position is? Stand in front of a mirror and note how much more informal and open you look with your coat or blazer unbuttoned.

Notice how people orient their centers when sitting at meetings. When two rival executives are placed in adjacent chairs, they will almost always sit with their shoulders angled away from each other, possibly with legs crossed so that their up foot points away from the unfriendly neighbor.

A child psychologist told me he always has both parents come with their child to the first meeting. He observes the parents in the lobby before the appointment. If the parents are sitting with their centers open, possibly with the husband's arm around his wife or at least turned toward each other, the psychologist spends most of the first meeting talking with the child. If the parents are closed to each other as they sit or do not sit next to each other, or if one of them sits with the child while the other sits across from the two, the psychologist spends his time probing to see if there are any problems between the parents that could be affecting the child.

The orientation of the center can also be used to control territorial space. While waiting in a bus station one snowy afternoon, I saw an attractive young woman walk over to one of the few places where there were several seats available and sit down, placing her luggage in front of her. She was immediately spied by one of the denizens of bus stations everywhere, a well-lubricated serviceman (who, like me, had been stranded by the snow). He staggered by the young woman and saw the empty seat next to her. Making as accurate a lunge as he could, he plopped down in the seat and lolled back, looking at her. She visibly tensed, but rather than leaving and risk embarrassing herself or the service-man, she turned away from him and stared off into another part of the lobby. The serviceman got the message and wandered off for more friendly game. (The young woman noticed some other potential nuisances and put her baggage in the seat next to her to ward off anybody else.)

We can be threatened by an open center when standing next to a stranger. As Figure 4-2 shows, opening our center intensifies our need for territorial space.

A short comment about the crossed-arms method of closing off the center is needed here. Most books report that this is al-ways a negative sign. One researcher went so far as to suggest that it had to do with a teenage girl's embarrassment at her devel-oping chest. Having never been a young woman going through puberty (nor was the researcher), I can't really verify or support this theory. It also does not account for why men do it.

I believe that crossed arms is an overrated sign. Often, it is just a comfortable thing to do with our arms, probably started by

SECURE

Closed — Closed

THREATENING

Neutral — Open

NORMAL

Neutral — Neutral

NORMAL

Neutral — Open

Figure 4–2. Public centers.

one of Tarzan's friends' ancestors and picked up by everyone else with a decent set of arms. I saw an incident that reinforced my opinion when I was downtown shopping during Christmas. A woman was standing at a bus stop with her three-year-old daughter. The mother was posed impatiently, weight shifted to one foot, arms crossed, and an exasperated expression on her face. As I walked down the sidewalk, I saw the little girl, who was standing in the rumpled manner of little people everywhere, look up and study her mother. Glancing quickly back and forth from her own body to her mother's, she slowly crossed her arms, shifted her weight, and when she was certain she "had it right" stood triumphantly with the same imperious look her mother showed. That was proof enough for me of where the crossed-arm gesture comes from and what it means when taken by itself. More than most other NVC signs, it means *nothing.*

Center orientations can also indicate people's relationships in groups. In Figure 2–1, for example, the "choir effect" and "outsider" configurations were indicated by people's centers as well as by their territorial space. The three subordinates encircling the leader all had their centers oriented to the boss. The person "out" of the informal circle was closed off by the people on either side. As you become more aware of centers, you will be able to read people's open and closed attitudes toward others, and their aggressive and submissive attitudes about themselves.

Head

It's rod time again. Imagine a rod going through that open alley your friends claim connects your ears. Then imagine another rod going straight back into your head through the tip of your nose. If you can picture these rods providing an axis of rotation for the head, you can see how the head can nod up and down around the first rod and tilt left and right about the second. As Figure 4–3 shows, the ear rod is your self line, and the nose rod is your others line.

By rotating about these lines, the head can assume four basic positions. If the head is rotated upward around the self line, you

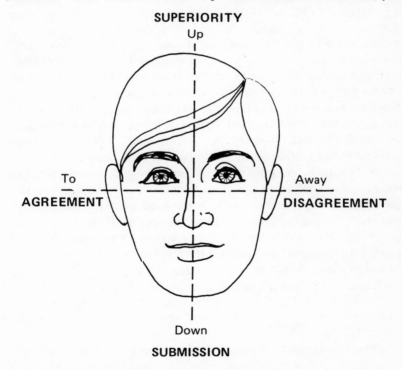

Figure 4–3. Head positions.

are showing *superiority* ("looking down your nose" at someone). William F. Buckley frequently appears to hold this position. If your head rotates downward, you are showing *submission* ("hanging your head"). If your head is tilted around the others line toward someone, you are indicating *agreement.* If it is tilted away, you are indicating *disagreement.*

As Figure 4–4 shows, these head positions can be used in combination during a conversation. At first, the boss is offering criticism in a very concerned manner. When the subordinate responds in too submissive a fashion, the boss returns to a dominant approach. This sparks rebellion in the subordinate and they are both off to the interpersonal races.

Tilting the head with the center open can indicate other things besides agreement. Often it is a sign of *attention.* (Remember King Kong holding Fay Wray with his head tilted, thinking, "Hmm"?) Many people unconsciously tilt their head when they are trying to listen more closely (listening with an "ear cocked"). The tilt can also be a sign of *evaluation* or *deep thought.* As we are thinking, we tilt our head and gaze into space with unfocused eyes while the brain churns. Or at least that's what we want people to think. I sometimes go through this "deep thought" routine after being asked a difficult question in a class. I may know the answer immediately, but my response will be more credible if I seem to be working for it. Besides, it is a compliment to the questioner to honor his or her query with such effort.

Watch how you position your head. Is your normal position neutral? Some of us assume a dominant or submissive position out of habit. As we saw in the section on height might, unconscious habits can influence the way people view us. One clerk I know habitually looks up at people. To my knowledge, he's still waiting for his first promotion. On the other hand, people resent those who have their "nose in the air." "Keep a level head about you" and watch when others don't.

FACIAL EXPRESSIONS

The syndicated column "Fables of the Famous" tells the story about the French novelist Balzac's first visit to Vienna. He was not familiar with either the language or the money and was

MANAGER: *"Your work has not been up to par."*

SECRETARY: *"I'm sorry."*

MANAGER: *"It's not good enough just to be sorry."*

SECRETARY: *"Well, it's not my fault!"*

Figure 4–4. Conversation head positions.

afraid he was being overcharged whenever he traveled by taxi. To make certain that he would not be "taken" on his trips, he developed a simple payment procedure based on the driver's face. Upon arriving, he would hand the driver a single coin. If the driver's hand remained out expectantly, he would add another coin. He kept adding one at a time until the driver smiled. Then Balzac would take back the last coin and depart, confident that he had paid the proper fare and no more!

Our face is the most expressive part of our body—something Balzac's drivers clearly didn't know. Birdwhistell estimated that we can make and recognize nearly 250,000 distinct facial expressions. Most researchers recognize the following as the most common:

> Interest/excitement
> Enjoyment/joy
> Surprise/startlement
> Distress/anguish
> Shame/humiliation
> Contempt/disgust
> Anger/rage
> Fear/terror

Instead of showing these various expressions during the working day, most people wear "masks." Retail clerks have their die-cast smiles and sales personnel have their hearty personalities, no matter how bad the day has been. An old saying warns, "Beware of someone who laughs without a shaking belly." We can mask with muscular control (poker face) or with a prop (toupee, wig, or colored contact lenses). We can choose to accentuate certain characteristics that overshadow others, like Jimmy Durante always posing in profile. (No one seems to have ever noticed the color of Jimmy Durante's eyes.)

When we do show emotions, we often display them in *partials*, reacting with only a portion of the face. I had a regional manager who was the most unconvincing liar I have ever met. He frightened everybody in the office because whenever he praised our sales, he smiled only with his mouth. When he told us how much better we were going to do next year (or else), he showed it with his entire face.

Sometimes we let our emotions out in uncontrollable "flashes." I was sitting at my desk one afternoon when someone from outside the sales office came in to use the phone. I glanced up and, not recognizing the woman, went back to my work. She caught my glance and said, "Well, hi, Ken. I haven't seen you for quite a while."

I looked up again, still not recognizing her, until her voice told me who she was: a customer I had not seen for nearly 18 months. My confusion arose because when I had seen her last, she had carried about 380 pounds on a 5'2" frame. I had been to her company five times before I ever saw her stand up. The woman I was looking at must have weighed 200 pounds less. Being the cool, suave, controlled NVC expert that I am, I let my jaw drop and managed an unintelligible, "Huh? Wha? Joan?" It took nearly a minute for the shock to pass and my brain to associate the new Joan with the old version in memory. I later apologized for acting so stupid, but she told me, "Don't worry about it, Ken. It's the nicest compliment you could have paid me. Besides, I like to see salesmen speechless occasionally." This was a pleasant, but rather unnerving flash.

Flashes can be negative too, as shown in the famous (and true) High School Reunion Story:

"Well, hon, I sure am looking forward to going to my reunion and seeing how everyone has turned out," Bill told his wife.

"You go by yourself. I'm eight months pregnant and look horrible. I can't sleep, I'm uncomfortable, and the clothes I have hang on me like a sheet."

"Okay, if that's the way you want it, Nancy. I really wanted to go to find out what happened to two old flames I had, one of whom was particularly flamy."

"I'll go, I'll go, you rat. But this is going to cost you a dress!"

Once at the reunion, Bill eagerly looked for his old girl friends without success. Later, while Nancy sat at a table with friends, Bill walked over to talk to some old football buddies. As Bill turned to leave the group, a woman came up and said, "Well, how are you, Bill?" Noticing the confused expression on his face, she continued, "You don't recognize me, do you?"

"Sure I do, Ruth. How are you?" Bill said carefully. He said it carefully because the version of Ruth he saw was carrying 70 more pounds than the attractive teenager he remembered. As they talked on, Bill patted himself on the back for not letting his jaw fall to the floor; then he heard something that told him he was still in trouble.

"I'd sure like to meet your wife," Ruth said.

"Here we go again," Bill thought. "I hope Nancy can hold her surprise too."

When Bill introduced Ruth to his wife, he could tell Nancy had no idea who she was talking to. Then, suddenly, Nancy did a slow pan to Bill with a widening smile.

"I knew Nancy had just gotten six months' worth of ammo," Bill told me later. "All I heard when I got home was, 'Haw, haw, haw. This,' Nancy said, pointing to her belly, 'will go away. That won't. Haw, haw, haw. Wait until I tell your mother.' "

At the reunion, had Bill and Nancy not been able to control their expressions, they could have easily embarrassed or hurt Ruth, just the opposite of what I did to Joan.

One of the reasons expression is so easy to read and difficult to control is that it is made up of eight different factors: forehead, brows, lids, eyes, nose, lips, chin, and skin.

Forehead

The forehead is a great indicator of physical and emotional states. A furrowed brow, read along with other facial features, can indicate puzzlement, deep thought, tension, worry, fear, or concern. A sweating forehead may indicate effort or nervousness. A naturally wide forehead or one due to a receding hairline often adds strength of character to the face. A small forehead or one hidden by hair gives a younger, more casual appearance.

Eyebrows

Eyebrows can be very expressive. They can be furrowed, heavy, light, penciled, soft, and a myriad of other adjectives spelled out in romantic novels. The brows tend to soften or harden a face. John F. Kennedy, for example, had what scientists call "medially downturned eyebrows," which gave his face a concerned look even at rest. Imagine JFK with Everett Dirksen's bushy eyebrows of down-to-earth experience. Thin, penciled eyebrows give a more mature, hardened look to a woman. Arched brows are more dramatic. Light eyebrows on either a man or a woman give the face a softer quality, lacking presence. The vertical line between the brows help form a concerned, worried look.

Eyebrow movement can indicate a variety of emotional states. Our brows may move up suddenly with surprise, fear, or recognition, or they may move down forcefully to indicate concern, worry, or anger. Richard Nixon's overhanging brows give him that brooding, sinister look that cartoonists love.

Eyelids

Eyelids are primarily indicators of alertness or involvement. People who have that sleepy or hooded look are thought to be cool, slow-moving, in control, and detached. An overlong gaze with lids lowered can show sexual interest. Bright-eyed, or wide-eyed people often have a look of alertness, innocence, or wonder. Examples of these two extremes are Charles Bronson and Eddie Cantor. Much of the "inscrutable Oriental" image is created by the epicanthic skin fold (sometimes called the Mongolian fold) around the eye, which gives it a more closed look.

The wink is a useful NVC device. It can mean "Okay" or "Hi, cute person," or it can be a warming personal gesture. Many of the modern "yuk and chuckle" newscasters make this their main tool for exhibiting warmth and charisma. A wink can leer if it is broad enough, or it can point out that the previous statement was sarcastic. A very long wink will almost guarantee a laugh from any crowd because it is a burlesque of the "smooth mover."

Eyes

Important as the eyelids, brows, and forehead are, they all pale in significance compared with the eyes. The eyes indeed have it. Often called "the windows of the soul," they indicate the object of our attention. You know how mad you get when someone wears dark glasses indoors? You are uncomfortable because the other person has the distinct advantage of being able to look anywhere unobserved. Dark glasses allow people to break the unwritten rules of eye contact.

By school age, most children have learned the basic rule of public eye contact: *civil inattention.* Throughout their early years, they have been told, "It's not polite to stare," "Don't look at that poor man while he's eating," or "Keep your eyes to yourself." Civil inattention is the habit of letting your gaze rest momentarily on someone before moving on after a decent period of time. That time can vary from group to group and situation to situation, but it is usually about one second long. As we walk along the sidewalk, our gaze will flicker randomly from face to face in civil inattention timespans, our expression never changing. At a party, civil inattention time is extended slightly as people size each other up.

If we look too long, we are guilty of *immoral looking time.* We can show interest or challenge someone by maintaining too much eye contact. If you walk along the same street resting your gaze for immoral looking times, you can cause people to avert their eyes. Or you may find others challenging your gaze by staring back belligerently as if to say (as in the battery commercial), "You want to start something?"

Sexual interest can also be shown by a lingering gaze. I was walking down the street one afternoon with a bachelor in our office when a young secretary from our building walked by. As we passed her, my friend stopped and turned around, watching her recede. When I asked what was going on, he told me to be quiet for a moment. When she was about 30 feet away, she glanced back over her shoulder, much to my friend's glee. I stood there confused as he exclaimed, "Got her!"

He explained as we walked away, "Whenever I see a good-looking woman walking toward me, I let my gaze linger over her and give her an appreciative smile as I go by. If I get a smile back, I stop to see if it's worth tracking her down. If she turns around, I give her another smile because now I *know* it's worth tracking her down." He had a date with her within two days.

We also practice the *cripple shift* on certain classes of people. One of my students, a woman paralyzed from the waist down and confined to a wheelchair, told me about the way people stare at her. The minute she catches people looking at her, they avert their eyes so "she won't think they are staring." Can you imagine going through life with people instantly looking away from you as you meet their eyes and then trying constantly to sneak a peek when they think you aren't looking? The most human thing to do is to practice civil inattention here too, letting your eyes rest for the normal moment before moving on.

The worst version of public eye contact is the *nonperson stare*. The nonperson stare does not grant the other person enough status to deserve civil inattention. It "looks right through us," as if we weren't there. Examples are the hate stare we give people we are prejudiced against and the blank stare we give waiters or waitresses as we talk at our table and watch them do their jobs. The blank look is a most outrageous insult.

Private looking time is vastly different from public looking time, because eye contact is expected to go up when we talk to people we know. The degree of eye contact in a conversation can often vary from 25 percent to 100 percent, depending on who is talking. Contact is reduced when we are doing the talking and is dramatically increased when we are listening—going from a normal 40 percent to 60 percent for talking to an average 80 percent for listening. Too much eye contact can again become dominating.

A manager I once knew maintained almost total eye contact whether he was speaking or listening. It was as if he came out of a basket to the tune of an Indian flute. If his eyes had spiraled, he could have starred as the snake in Disney's *Jungle Book*. Everyone was uncomfortable in his presence and felt intimidated in staring back at him or in trying to furtively look away. This manager was very tall and had a nonexistent intimate territorial space. Ten minutes with this man standing closely over you and staring into your eyes and you would have admitted to any heinous crime.

Too little eye contact shows a lack of strength or purpose. We have all talked to someone who wouldn't look us in the eye and come away feeling cheated, having no respect for that person. If the gaze moves too quickly we are also concerned, because the person is "shifty-eyed." I was talking to a reporter for a local TV station about a recent mayoral election. One of the candidates, a man running for office for the first time, hadn't learned to ignore the camera. When he was interviewed, he kept shifting his eyes from the reporter to the bright lights and whirring sound. After the interview, the reporter suggested he look at one or the other in the future, because the film was going to show him as a shifty-eyed politician. Unfortunately, there weren't any more interviews and the candidate lost in a landslide.

It's also disconcerting to talk to someone whose eyes are unfocused. This gives a confused, bubbleheaded look to any face. Excessive blinking and eye watering are other negative signs. Blinking makes us look nervous, and watery eyes make us seem overemotional or weak. Many contact lens wearers don't realize the real NVC price of their lenses, as they rub their eyes in discomfort and wipe away the tears with the ever present Kleenex. Other wearers adopt the "contact stare," blinking only when necessary. Often this gives the face a strained, inflexible look, with the eyes locked open like a Shields and Yarnell robot.

Make certain the windows to your soul aren't clouded, giving the wrong information to the people in your life who are looking in. Practice civil inattention with *everybody* no matter what a person's physical condition. Look people in the eye as you listen, and don't be afraid to look away as you talk, it's normal. Keep your eyes on your subject, and your attention will follow.

Nose

Some people can make a career out of a nose, like Jimmy Durante, Bob Hope, and Cyrano de Bergerac. To most of us, the best nose is one people don't notice. There are all types of noses: hawkish curved noses, pixie upturned noses, sharp pointed noses, flat boxer's noses, and noble Roman noses. (When my wife's doctor asked her, "When did you break your nose?" she helped him place his foot in his mouth with the answer, "I never have. I'm Italian!") Each of these is a stereotype that helps define our image regardless of our real personality. Some people find the stereotype so distasteful that they modify their noses. Most of us are content with what we have.

There is really very little to "read" about a nose other than the nostrils. We can be likened to rabbits, nostrils quivering in anticipation, or racehorses, nostrils flared with eagerness. Often we widen our nostrils in fear or anger. Nostrils can provide some information, but why should we pay attention to them with what is waiting below?

Lips

Lips are one of the really interesting parts of the body. Humorist Richard Armour devoted an entire essay to Sophia Loren's lower lip. (I shudder to think how long he would have had to write had he expanded his study.) Lips are also the source of our aggression. "I'm going to give you a busted lip!" "Don't give me any lip!" "Why don't you keep your trap shut?" We even judge character from lips.

Lips can be full or thin. Full lips make a man or a woman look softer, warmer, and more sensual. Thin-lipped women frequently apply their lipstick outside of the lipline to give them a more sensual look. People with thin lips, such as Jack Lord in *Hawaii Five-O*, show more strength, firmness, coldness, and less emotion. Who wants to woo a thin-lipped lover, much less let a career depend on a tight-lipped manager?

Children often thrust their lower lips out in angry defiance. Grown-up lips can pout with petulance or sneer with superiority. (It is my greatest regret as an NVC consultant that I have the right-side sneer, and the "Yech!" double sneer, but I have been unable to develop the left-side sneer.) Lips can also drool with idiocy, part with promise, smirk with certainty, be bitten with nervousness, be licked with worry or anticipation, and have a host of other interesting movements not particularly pertinent to a business book. One of the most common things they do is smile.

Smiling frequency is a learned cultural trait. People in some areas of the country, primarily the South, smile more than others. Studies have shown that Atlanta, Memphis, Nashville, and Louisville residents smile the most. Where do people smile the least? While I resist drawing any editorial conclusions, people in New York smile less than those in any other city.

Every face has a *resting position*. This is the expression we have when our face is in "neutral," not showing any spontaneous or controlled emotion. (This is not a poker face, when we are trying to mask our feelings.) As we work, a large amount of time our face is expressionless (or so we think). Some people have a built-in smile or frown at the corners of their mouths. A vertical line at the lip corners also gives the impression of smiling frequently. As my customer from Chapter 1 who covered his mouth when listening knew, heavy facial lines running from the nose to the edge of the lips give a deep frown. All these resting positions affect how we look to others in our unguarded moments.

As you walk outside or around your building during lunch hour, start watching the faces of the people you pass. You may be surprised to find that the majority have a frowning position. The ones with a truly neutral look or the ones with pleasant expressions will appear much more friendly and warm. Which one are you?

Our lips may adopt a nonresting position when we are emotionless. One of the most difficult distractions I have ever faced in class came when a beautiful woman attended one of my sessions. She was the type that could stop conversation in the company cafeteria when she went through the line. She was very attentive in class, and it was hard to give the other students equal eye contact until I discovered a strange lip movement she had. As she listened, she would run her tongue over her gums as if cleaning her teeth after a big meal. It was not a sexy movement at all, just an earnest tongue polishing her teeth. I told a female associate of mine that I finally had the beauty in one of my sessions and she was driving me crazy! The response was an unsympathetic "I guess that's like marrying Farrah Fawcett-Majors and finding out she snores." Any one of the "active mouth" habits could be worse than a frown.

Chin

The chin is often considered an indicator of personal strength. Whenever we have problems we have to "take it on the chin." Westerns are full of square-jawed young heroes teaming up with lantern-jawed ex-sheriffs to stop those cowardly jowly outlaws. "Faced" with the big gunfight, the old-timer pats us on the shoulder and tells us, "Keep your chin up, kid, these skunks will scatter at the first shot!" We stroke our chin thoughtfully and reply, "Quit jawing at me, pops. I ain't scared." Sticking our jaw out defiantly, we stride off throwing the parting comment over our shoulder, "Besides, I'm going first." This whole important exchange would never have been possible without that wonderful device that holds our lower set of teeth.

The shape and position of the jaw help form our image. Square or angular jawlines are associated with strength; rounded jawlines are associated with warmth and openness. John Wayne, Clint Eastwood, and Kirk Douglas all show strength. Dick van Patton, Dom DeLuise, and Bill Cosby appear more open and people-oriented. Jacqueline Kennedy Onassis shows an angular strength, while Shirley Booth shows her warmth.

The jutting chin can create an aggressive, defiant look. The receding chin suggests meekness or lack of character. It is such a negative factor that it is often used for comic effect.

The skin around the chin is also important. Loose, jowly skin under and around the chin softens the personality and can even suggest weakness. Former Senator Sam Ervin's chin reinforced his easygoing slow-country-lawyer image. On women, this feature often contributes to a warm, grandmotherly image.

In general, the chin is not an item you can "read" for personality information. Instead, you should be aware of what the chin contributes to your image and the impressions you get from others.

Skin
One of the most common things skin does is get red, or blush. This uncontrollable burst of color across our face is a dead giveaway when we are embarrassed or self-conscious. In general, the easier we blush, the less strength and authority we appear to have. This is unfortunate, since blushing is largely an uncontrollable event, usually aggravated by some noxious co-worker who loves the power of being able to visibly embarrass someone. There is no way to "poker face" a blush. We immediately let other people know they have scored.

In addition to color, our skin shows physical depth and firmness. Thin-skinned people, literally and emotionally, appear sensitive, gentle. You have to approach them with finesse and care. Thick-skinned people are tough, in control, and hearty. You can be more direct with them, more open and blunt. They admire forceful, aggressive people. It's tougher to "get under their skin."

Our skin can appear firm and tight or soft and droopy. Romantic literature is full of phrases such as "skin stretched tautly over high cheekbones beneath intense gray eyes" and "bulbous cheeks bouncing hideously as he tore at the turkey leg." Much like the loose skin around the chin, loose facial skin projects a soft personality. Firm skin connotes strength and, taken to the extreme, can indicate a nervous temperament.

Wrinkles are another frequent negative. An article in the December 8, 1977, issue of the *St. Louis Post-Dispatch*, noted that President Carter had wrinkled considerably since his election. The comments ran from Vice President Mondale's "I wish he had more time to completely relax" to Atlanta lawyer Charles Kirbo's "I think he is aging." Commonly thought of as one of the hardest-working Presidents in recent years, Carter was described in the article as "an American executive with workaholic tendencies."

The photo on the left in Figure 4–5 shows President Carter during the campaign; the photo on the right shows him in office. The "new look" Carter was said to have "strain . . . etched in his face and around his eyes." Although the lighting is different in the two pictures, in the later photo the President's brow is fur-

Figure 4–5. President Carter's wrinkles.
(Wide World Photos)

rowed; there are deeper valleys around the eyes and mouth and loose flesh under the chin. This important change in image may hurt President Carter unfairly, since the article also points out that the President's physician pronounced him "in better health than when he entered the White House."

Facial changes can also affect your image of success. You can minimize them by careful emphasis on other features.

HAIRSTYLES AND ACCESSORIES

Hairstyles can play an important role in shaping people's image. John Molloy recommends that men wear their hair like the men in authority they deal with, and that women wear neat styles of medium length without excessive wave or curl. For example, men calling on executives who wear short hair should also wear their hair short. Don't be like long-haired comedian Ricky Jay, who observed, "I perform for people who have spent their entire lives working to earn enough money to get away from people who look like me." This works in reverse too. A friend of mine who is a reservist, and thus has to wear his hair short, worked as a salesman calling on "head shops" (retail stores specializing in drug paraphernalia). Even though he wore appropriate clothes (jeans), store owners were reluctant to trust him and buy from him. He finally had to buy a wig.

In general for men, the shorter the hair, the more conservative the look. The most conservative style is the crewcut. For women, the longer the hair, the more feminine the look; the shorter the style, the more conservative. Hair color can also contribute to people's image. While blonds may have more fun socially, brunettes are considered more authoritative.

Baldness frequently makes a man look more powerful and authoritative. Look at Mr. Clean, Kojak, Daddy Warbucks, and Yul Brynner as the King of Siam. Total baldness is best for showing power. The effect is lost somewhat when there is a halo of hair on the sides or when side hair is combed over the bald spot.

A toupee can have a mixed effect. First, it is an obvious show of vanity in a man, something America's "wooden Indian" concept of masculinity looks down on. It also can be a bad toupee. I remember seeing a graying man with a toupee in a restaurant. He looked like he was carrying a puppy on his head, because the toupee was the color of his long-lost brown hair with the gray showing at the bottom.

Sometimes a man will not be consistent in wearing his toupee. You may see him wearing it one day and several weeks later walk by a bald man without recognizing him. Consequently, the toupee becomes a source of distraction. On the positive side, a toupee is well worth the investment if the improvement in self-image causes a change in behavior for the better.

Facial hair also affects a man's image. One secretary told me that ever since the 1972 Olympics every young executive she sees looks like Mark Spitz. A mustache can make a young man look older, but it has a price. It is very difficult to counteract the natural frown a mustache gives a face, much like the painted frown on a circus clown. The farther away the viewer is, the less the lips appear to be smiling. If the mustache is too long, lunches can get very messy. It's difficult to be impressive with a drop of hamburger grease beading on your upper lip hair. A mustache that is too large, such as a handlebar or Pancho Villa style, can also detract from a man's appearance.

Chin hair is bad at best but should at least be neatly trimmed and fairly short. Long beards are out of style. A businessman wants to look dignified, like Sebastian Cabot, not shaggy, like Hopalong Cassidy's sidekick. Goatees are out, as are scraggly chin whiskers. Goatees just don't seem to look dashing enough without a turban or flowing robe, and lonesome chin whiskers are too goatlike for comfort.

At this writing, sideburns are supposedly going out after their time in the sun. I'm not sure they were *ever* in, considering the way top executives have ignored hairstyles. I may be prejudiced against sideburns, because I can't grow any (I just don't have the follicles). Still, I believe they fall under the category of detractors. The best sideburns are those that when asked of someone, "How long were his sideburns?" you reply, "I don't know; I never noticed." Most men don't want to look like Elvis, nor do they want to have a Little Rascals bowl cut.

Whatever your hairstyle, you should look neat at all times. There is no reason not to stop in a restroom before any important meeting to make an appearance check, particularly after lunch. Comedian Shelley Berman tells of coming home from an unfriendly date one evening to find a piece of spinach plastered on his front tooth. Going directly to any meeting after walking around outside gives us a disheveled nonprofessional look. Don't let it happen to you!

For those of you who are as blind as I am, glasses are a major head accessory. Although you may feel like you are looking at life through two toilet paper rolls, others observe your glasses as part of your image. In general, glasses make people appear more studious and can help give a face authority. This advantage can be reduced, though, if you wear glasses with oversized lenses, flashy colored frames, or those designer glasses with distracting initials on the frame. I wear goggle-shaped wire rims, one size above normal and have been told that they make me look older. For men, heavy plastic or horn rims can have the same effect (although they don't provide as big a field of vision). Glasses can be a big asset for women because they often create a more businesslike and authoritative image. Fashion frames or greatly oversized lenses will undo this advantage, as will half-glasses worn down the nose in the "granny" look.

On the body movement scan, notice a person's head position and features. The position and expression will give you an indication of how people feel about themselves and others, and the hairstyle and accessories will help you analyze their images.

Posture

Posture is very closely related to the center. Stooping closes off the center and pulling the shoulders back makes the center aggressive. *Stooped* or *bowed* shoulders can mean many things, all negative. You may be burdened, self-conscious, unconfident, submissive, beaten, guilty, or afraid. *Retracted* shoulders may make you appear insensitive, angry, impulsive, belligerent, domineering, or mean on the negative side. Depending on your other scan signs, you may also appear forceful, confident, firm, tenacious, and authoritative. *Raised* shoulders usually show tension or even apprehension and fear. *Squared* shoulders generally suggest strength and responsibility.

Have you ever caught yourself driving home from work with your shoulders hunched up around your ears? You probably thought, "I didn't realize I was this tense. I think I'll relax." You drive along a little farther and reflect, "Gee, that worked once. I wonder if it will work again?" So you relax your shoulders a little more. I have driven home from a tough sales day and done that four different times. Each time I thought I was fully relaxed at last, but with the tension of the day and of the evening rush-hour traffic, I couldn't relax all at once. Many of us spend a good deal of our day in this posture, transmitting our worry and tension to the entire office with our shoulders.

Leaning is another facet of posture. The way people lean often indicates how they feel about others. Generally, leaning backward is negative and leaning forward is positive. ("I'm leaning *toward* capital punishment.") When juicy gossip hits the lunchroom table, you can see people lean forward with interest. You go into your boss's office to ask for a raise and the boss leans back in the chair silently as you talk. Leaning affects height relationships. When we lean backward, we gain an artificial height might because we are now looking down at others, even if they are standing and we are sitting. If we lean forward, we pass the advantage to others or at least neutralize it, because we are level or looking up to them.

There is at least one advantage to leaning forward. I recently had a press release photograph taken for use with my seminars and articles. The photographer suggested I lean forward, looking the camera directly in the lens with head erect. Although my face is just so-so (I would rather look like Robert Redford), the pose gave me a more aggressive appearance.

Seating postures are also important. In general, the more relaxed we are when sitting, the higher our status. This makes it easy for Joe B. in Chapter 1 to pick out the Star and Heel in any group. We would never think of going into our boss's office, plopping down in the chair beside the desk in a comfortable slump, and saying, "Howya doin', super cheese?" The boss could easily do this to us, though. Superiority is also shown by relaxed postures such as feet on the desk (if it's your desk, the boss is crowding your territorial space and showing contempt for your possessions), lying back in the chair with hands behind head and legs crossed straight out in front, sitting on your desk (crowding with a height advantage), or sitting turned with a leg over the arm of the chair.

Your sense of presence and authority can also be increased by having what my portrait photographer called a "solid base." He told me that too many PR pictures are posed so that the subject looks like an anvil sitting on a TV tray. He positioned me in a chair turned just slightly away from the camera with my elbows out and hands placed midway down my thighs. This way, my figure was narrowest at the head, angled down to the shoulders, and then angled wider below the shoulders because of the arm position. No part of the background showed through under the arms to spoil the base. A courtroom judge benefits from this look because of the flowing robe. Any clothing of this type—a toga, a dashiki, or a flowing evening gown—adds to our image by solidifying our posture.

Hands

There are four basic areas of the hand: tips, palm, edge, and back. Hand motions involving tips are usually emphatic, as in "making a point." We discipline our children by shaking our finger at them or poking them in the chest. As we turn to leave, they shoot us in the back with the index-finger barrel of their "handgun" smoking in their imagination. At the Cotton Bowl in Texas fans cheer their Longhorns using the famous "hook 'em horns" gesture, with index finger and little finger extended. Uncle Sam looked us in the eye, pointed his finger, and emphatically let us know, "I want *you!*"

Showing the palm is a friendly, peaceful motion. Historians speculate that it originated when people extended their hands on meeting to show they had no weapons. At the altar, the Catholic priest extends his arms, turns his palms out, and intones, "Go in peace, the mass is ended." The rock star acknowledges the cheers of the youthful crowd by waving hands over head with palms out. We wave in greeting; the Indian greets us with steady palm out. The *Star Trek* writers gave Mr. Spock the Vulcan version of the Indian greeting with second and third fingers parted.

Edge-of-hand gestures are very forceful, like karate chops. They add sharp, quick bursts of punctuation to our movements. We wave away a thought we disagree with, we strike the table with the edge of our clenched fist. We use the edge of our hand much like a sword, slicing horizontally and vertically to defend or attack.

The back of the hand shows vitality. It can be aggressive, unfriendly, or negative. The forceful edge-of-hand black-power salute becomes "shaking your fist" at someone just by turning the hand so that the back is out. Nelson Rockefeller showed us the older generation can learn from the young when a photographer caught him with his middle finger thrust defiantly upward at hecklers. The same gesture is not nearly offensive enough if it is given palm out—try it in a mirror and see. In Britain Churchill's victory sign, known the world over, becomes the equivalent of our one-finger gesture if it is shown with the back of the hand outward. We express disbelief by touching our fingertips to our chest and saying, "Who me?"

A closed fist is the universal sign of force. It is rarely positive in a business environment, where it can signal anger, disagreement, fear, frustration, or power. We often employ the fist for emphasis, using it to pound our palm, pound the desk, or pound the other person. A modified version of this requires wearing a ring. An evening student of mine who is on active duty with the Army told me about certain officers known as "ring pounders." These are service academy graduates who seem to develop the habit of pounding the flat of their hand, the one with the graduation ring, on the desk as they speak. It is irritating to the men but helps the officers dominate any meeting they are in.

The service academy ring is a good example of using jewelry to advantage. In general, any hand jewelry other than wedding band and watch can be detrimental to your gestures. Any jewelry that makes noise, such as a bracelet, is reason for justifiable homicide by your fellow workers. One day with a jangling bracelet wearer is enough to make you want to lop off both his or her hands. Your watch should fit your wrist snugly, so that it doesn't bang around. As a side comment, the wedding band can be a plus for both men and women because it reduces the number of "on the make" encounters. Some women wear a band even though they are not married, just to take the social pressure off in business situations. (An attractive friend tells me the only sure way to deflate the incessant wolf is to state, "I only date certain types of people. Are you saved?") Married executives may think they are clever by taking off their wedding ring for business trips, but most single people I know have learned to look at the ring finger carefully. If it has had a ring on it regularly, the finger will show an indentation. (The best way to hide it is to put another ring over it.) In general, additional rings should be kept to a minimum. I wear only a wedding band and an athletics-related college ring. More than one per hand most likely will detract from your business image rather than add to it.

Legs

Although we spend a large amount of our business time sitting, we also have to stand and communicate, if only at the water cooler. A wide stance with feet spread apart is very masculine. We can picture the coach coming out, stopping with a wide base, putting his hands on his hips, and yelling, "Everybody in the pool!" A narrow stance is very feminine. Models are taught to stand with their feet gracefully brought together in a modified T. Imagine the coach coming out, putting his hands on his hips with feet in the dainty T, and mincing, "Okay, now, let's jump in that pool!" Or imagine a woman walking out at the fashion show, and stopping with feet widely placed in the "ten minutes to two" position. This is often considered to be a "loose woman" pose.

We can also interpret how people position their legs when sitting. In almost every tense situation, such as an appraisal or a job interview, a man will cross his ankles in front of him. A woman will usually cross them under the chair. Crossed ankles are a readiness sign, showing self-control. Crossed legs, on the other hand, are a sign of unreadiness, or nonconcurrence. For women, this means the leg-over-leg position; for men, the ankle-on-opposite-knee or "figure 4" position. For some unknown reason, we rarely make a decision when one foot is off the floor.

A special case of leg position is walking. Are you a wall hugger? Then you probably create the impression of being shy and diffident, because you are giving ground and making it easier for others to pass. (Americans hug the right wall and the English hug the left.) Aggressive, dominant people walk down the middle of the hallway, making others push to the side to pass by. If they come face to face with someone, they stop and make the other person step aside so they can pass.

Many NVC experts read too much into walking. One book claims that a springy, bouncy walk shows enthusiasm and a high energy level. I walk this way, but there are many days I'm not too enthusiastic. Essentially, if we walk with our eyes and center, the feet will follow. The first two indicators are more important than the feet.

Women and men who wear high-heeled or platform shoes should realize what they are doing to themselves and their walk.

Figure 4–6. High-heeled walking.

There is a reason why their walk is so clunky, and why they have to take little steps. The high heels force an unnatural motion of the heel. Look at Figure 4–6, showing a bare foot stepping down. When the heel touches the floor, it does not move until after the foot has rotated flat. The heel finally rises off the ground as the weight is shifted forward for the next step.

In a high-heeled shoe the foot must continue to move after the shoe heel touches the floor because of its distance from the ground. As the foot rotates flat, the heel moves forward nearly two inches for a three-inch heel. The heel then rises normally for the next step. The only way to reduce the extra two-inch arc is to take smaller steps and come down nearly flatfooted, causing the clunky high-heeled walk. There is no way to walk normally in high heels. For image reasons alone (ignoring the ankle injuries), no businessperson should make very high heels a part of his or her wardrobe.

Summary

This chapter introduced the third NVC checklist, one that helps you evaluate body features and movements. As you observe others, ask yourself:

1. Are people open or closed, aggressive or submissive? (CENTER)
2. What do their head positions, facial expressions, and features show? (HEAD)
3. How do they hold themselves? (POSTURE)
4. What type of gestures are they using? (HANDS)
5. What are their feet doing? (LEGS)

You now have the information you need to systematically read and evaluate someone's NVC. With practice, you can quickly scan body location, surroundings, and body features and movements head to toe. You can also begin to better control your own NVC to improve your business image. To be fully prepared for this, you need to take a more detailed look at gestures.

5

Interpreting Gestures

Arms and hands are second only to the face in expressiveness. They can tell stories in a hula dance or transmit detailed "speech" to the deaf. They can provoke a fight or start a crowd screaming or laughing. They can summon the waiter with a check or control a postgame traffic jam.

Many vocations have special gestures. When I was a rod man on a survey crew during the summers, I learned a complete set of hand signals from the transit man (walkie-talkies were not popular then). If I was not holding the rod vertical, he would put both hands over his head palms together and lean in the direction he wanted me to straighten the rod. If I was laying stakes off line, he would point to the side I should move. The faster his arm pointed and returned to his side, the smaller the distance I should move.

Deep-sea diving, another environment where speech is useless, also has a gesture language for standard or expected situations. Thumbs up or down means ascend or descend. You point in the horizontal direction you wish to go. If you point to your watch, you are indicating it is time to surface because of dwindling air supply. If you point to your compass, you are asking, "Which way next?" A hand extended palm up means, "What next?" Emergency signals include clutching your neck, running your hand knifelike across your throat, removing your mouthpiece, and pointing to your regulator.

Standard Gestures

Standard social gestures are called *emblems*. The hitchhiker stands at the roadside shaking an extended fist with thumb out. If something is satisfactory, we signal okay by putting our thumb and index finger together in a circle. The peace sign is given with palm out and index and second finger extended. For a time, the peace sign was a greeting signal between the young, replacing the wave or handshake.

It seems like every winning football squad on New Year's Day runs off the field with index fingers proclaiming, "We're No. 1." We indicate other numbers by raising up the proper number of fingers. If the number is higher than 5, we open and close the hand for the proper multiple of 5 and give the partial hand count at the end.

We also have gestures that show pictures. I always ask for the check at a restaurant by catching the eye of the waiter and drawing a square in the air with my finger. I have never had this sign misinterpreted. Men often describe a remarkable female shape by tracing the appropriate curves in the air in front of them. Women may similarly describe a man's V-shaped chest. (I have a deep H myself.) We may diagram a football play on our hand or describe the route to our office by tracing the directions on the desk.

I once made a silent movie to be used as a coffeebreak film at a large regional computer sales meeting. An associate of mine played Charlie Chaplin's Little Tramp, and I played a typical young salesman in the early 1900s. One scene called for us to watch an old-time card sorter in action. At the last minute, we were unable to come up with an old enough machine, so we played the scene in pantomime. I walked up to an empty space and proudly pointed out the machine with a wave of my hand. Then I carefully removed the imaginary large cover and folded it up. I gave a brief explanation of the various parts of the machine and loaded in the cards. We were worried that the mature business audience wouldn't accept this bit of make-believe. It turned out the gestures were more than sufficient to capture the audience's imagination, and the film was one of the highlights of the meeting.

Other standard gestures show space relationships. The most common is the fish story. The erstwhile Captain Ahab describes his battle with a Maybe Big Fish, arms getting farther apart with each retelling. We can't seem to keep from giving space relationships even if we are talking about the near miss in the parking lot, or coming "this close" (holding finger and thumb two inches apart) to blowing up at a subordinate. When I tell my classes about my encounter with Mike, the man with no intimate space, (Chapter 2), I always hold up my hand with thumb and little finger extended saying, "this far" to indicate how close our faces were. So the audience realizes how close that really is, I then pick out some poor unfortunate, put my thumb to my nose, and move up until my little finger is almost touching the subject's nose.

We often use gestures to mimic others. A successful insurance agent I know sells seemingly on raw instinct. There is little relationship between his approach and any information the potential client gives him. Still, he has an uncanny success rate of calls to sales. As we were talking about this one night, I asked him to describe his last sales call that day. As he talked about the sequence of events, he began to unconsciously act out the parts. I was seeing a stage version of his sales call. He was able to notice and use the NVC the clients gave him, but better yet he remembered their actions and could apply them in later calls. As the night wore on, I realized that he had to re-create the movements of each customer to be able to tell me about the sale.

We all are natural mimics to some extent; otherwise, we would never have learned to walk or talk. You can watch two people from across the office and often tell what they are talking about by their movements. The storyteller will "conduct" the story in addition to telling it, sometimes performing the solo parts too.

Gestures can be used to trace the flow of a discussion or to list the main points of an argument. We summarize a discussion where we give both points of view with an open palm turned upward ("On the one hand . . . on the other . . ."). The opposing points are counted on the fingers of each hand. We can even tell which side a person is defending by the hand that is used. A right-handed person usually reserves the favored point of view for the right hand; the reverse is true for the left-hander. You can tell which hand a person usually uses by the watch. Except for the small percentage of left-handers, most people wear their watch on the left hand, a fact that has kept mystery writers in plot clues for years.

Touching

We reveal how we feel in many situations by touching ourselves and others. Some touching gestures are important indicators; others are mannerisms that have outlived their usefulness. Rich Little, one of the few comedians to "do" Johnny Carson, told how hard it was to develop a Carson impression. Watching Carson's monologues for several shows, he counted over 20 self-touching mannerisms that were part of Carson's regular delivery —smoothing the coat, touching the face with index finger, straightening the tie, and so on. Although many of these gestures are associated with nervousness, Carson claims that he is not really nervous anymore; he makes the gestures because he is keyed up for each monologue.

I became aware of two unconscious mannerisms of mine when I went out for track in college. Because the frames of my glasses interfered with my vision when I high-jumped, I switched to contacts for workouts and meets. During practice, I found myself punching my forehead between my eyebrows with my middle finger. I also put my hand over my face and grabbed my temples with my thumb and ring finger. I kept wondering why I was doing this, and I'm sure the other jumpers were concerned too. It finally occurred to me that I was pushing up my nonexistent glasses. I had gotten into the habit of doing it unconsciously and had not bothered to let my brain know that I was no longer wearing glasses.

We all have these useless little motions. I'm more aware of some of mine because my college students frequently use me as the subject of their NVC term project. I wipe chalk off my clean hands, push my glasses up my nose even if they are already up, rub the skin on my left hand where a steel splinter resided for several years, and more. I can only hope none of these manner-isms is too distracting to my classes. My students, however, know how to "drive me up a wall," sometimes purposely. My favorite villains are pen clickers, pencil tappers, plastic food wrap fondlers, head scratchers, and face contortionists. One dou-ble-jointed student used to absent-mindedly bend her index finger *backward* and touch the back of her hand. It made my hands ache to watch.

Touching is a repressed mannerism in our society. A study of conversations in outdoor cafés in several countries confirmed our reserved British heritage. Four cities were observed for touches (self or others) per hour of conversation. The results were San Juan, 180 per hour; Paris, 110 per hour; Gainesville, Florida, 2 per hour; and London, 0 per hour. Touching is restricted in our society because certain areas of the body, on ourselves or others are considered taboo. Until recently, married couples portrayed on TV weren't even allowed to sleep in the same bed. Greetings were confined to gentle busses on the cheek when the husband came home from work. Today there is a little more realism in the way married people are portrayed.

In a social or business setting with friends, certain portions of the body are touchable. The order of the most acceptable to least acceptable areas for women are hands and forearms, upper arms and top of head, head and shoulders and feet, and finally torso and legs. For men it is hands, shoulders and arms, top of head and upper body and legs, and finally lower body.

Every woman has experienced an unwanted male hand rest-ing softly on her shoulder. Many men have also encountered female associates whose constant touching makes them feel un-comfortable. With strangers, we prefer no touching. Notice how salesclerks will jerk their hand back if they accidentally touch a customer's hand while returning change. Observe how people will stand as far apart as possible on a crowded bus or elevator, shrinking back from each other even as they are forced together. Unwanted touching is the ultimate indignity to territorial space needs.

Socially, every man knows that he must overcome the touch-ing inhibitions of a new date. If you have ever broken up with a "steady" and then started dating again, you know how strange a new person "feels" on the first date. The clever bachelor will take every opportunity to contact those acceptable areas to acclimate the woman to his touch. He will help her on with her coat and linger at the shoulders, he will usher her through doors with gentle pressure on the small of her back or shoulders, and he will hold her hand or arm as they walk. I have many testimonials from men that this speeds intimacy, and many women students have in retrospect recognized this technique.

Professionally, men should never touch men other than with a handshake. The handshake is really nothing more than a toned-down embrace. Many a deal has been killed by the hearty back-slap. I don't like business associates punching, pushing, grabbing, or slapping. Generally, men touch men only in sports situations. I remember the crowd reaction when professional football teams started holding hands in the huddle. The crowd was giggly, and you could see that half the players really didn't want to do it. They just wanted to keep their job. Much more acceptable is the massive pile of hands before the game as players gather in a circle and break with a shout of "Let's go!" Strangely, the most accepted form of touch among men is the congratulatory slap on the rump. (Imagine being slapped on the rump by your boss after a good presentation.) Women seem at ease touching their own rear, as in the skirt-smoothing motion. Men would rather have another man do it. The man-to-man seat swat in sports can mean "Good job," "Too bad," "Better luck next time," or "Howya doin'?"

It is better in our society to touch objects. Cigarettes are a common touchable. Most smokers who have tried to quit realize their psychological dependence on the physical ritual surrounding smoking. Stop-smoking clinics suggest that people keep cigarettes in a different location so they become conscious of reaching for them, and that they avoid situations where they habitually smoke. Since the main point is having something in their mouths, and since thumb sucking is socially unacceptable, nonsmokers have had to turn to other objects. The number of chewed pencils in offices would embarrass the beaver population of the world. (I also hope the plastic pens are nontoxic.) We chew the ears on our glasses and nibble on toothpicks, letter openers, or cuticles and fingernails when we can sneak them. I'm always amazed by the number of people I see chomping away on their fingernails as they drive home from work. Mangled fingernails, a tribute to our high-pressure work world, may be the first symptom of ulcers.

Capitalizing on this need to handle something other than ourselves or our associates, fondle factories have produced a variety of touchables. If Captain Queeg can have his marbles, executives can have their paperweights, trophies, toy awards, doodle pads, Rube Goldberg phone directories, and giant erasers. (Ever notice how the giant erasers get dirty long before they are even slightly used?)

One reason jewelry is so popular is that it has a high fondle value. Twirling a bracelet or ring is satisfying and reassuring. Many businessmen who wear vests carry an old railroad watch on a chain instead of a wristwatch. They make a big production of pulling out the watch, snapping open the cover, and noting the time. This is much more elegant than turning the wrist slightly to look at the LEDs shining at you. With some of the more expensive electronic watches, you have to push the stem to see the time. Even though it is impossible to sneak a look at these watches, they sell well, because of their enhanced fondle value.

All these touching signs in our culture are good indicators that a person is seeking reassurance. They can also hint at nervousness, insecurity, lack of self-confidence, impatience, or fear.

Anticipation

One of the most common gestures of anticipation is the open palm of someone expecting a tip. This is often used by only the most aggressive of tipees, the bellhop. Bellhops must get shorted often, because they are so insistent when it comes to receiving a "gratuity." Rather than regarding a tip as an act of appreciation, they turn it into a bribe to make them leave before guilt or irritation overwhelms us.

Waiters often use a more subtle approach. They probably get shorted as frequently as bellhops, but they are much more civil. They linger by your table as you get up, so that if you don't leave a tip, you know that they know it. (All this time you thought they were just being friendly, hanging around to say good-by as you walked away.) If you use a credit card, the pushy waiter will look over the charge slip as he picks it up, so he can register his pleasure or muted disgust. ("Oh, *thank* you, sir.") A classy operator will merely glance at it to see that it has been signed, and then return your copy.

Another sign of anticipation is the prayer hand position, with palms rubbing back and forth as if to roll out a piece of dough. Without this typical gesture, arch villain Snidely Whiplash could have been played by R2D2. No self-respecting villain would ever snatch even the most insignificant deed out of the freezing widow's grasp without a little gleeful hand rubbing. Diners sometimes make this gesture as they first sight and smell their meal. In a meeting, some executives will "tip their hand" by making this gesture when they are about to jump on a mistake. During a sales presentation, I saw that one of the managers was going to break in with just such a point, so I stopped and said to his boss, who had a puzzled look, "You had a question?" By the time the boss was done, the manager's point was no longer pertinent and somewhat off the subject.

Anticipation also tends to increase the number and speed of our movements. The rhythm of people's gestures is tied to their speech patterns and emotional state. We need to become aware of any changes in this rhythm. A small child will jump up and down with excitement waiting in line for Santa. A teenage girl will run up and down the stairs and dart from bathroom to bedroom getting ready for that first date. Two parents may pace, fidget, or get into an argument waiting at the airport for their son to return home from the Army.

There are other, more superficial signs of anticipation. We cross our fingers to express hope (originally an early Christian religious sign) or to protect us from lying. We hold our hands together in prayer and look upward for guidance. We "knock on wood" to ward off any bad luck in mentioning how good life has been or what misfortune we have avoided.

A sharp intake of breath often indicates anticipation. The karate expert prepares for his blow and shout with a sharp breath.

Spectators at the circus collectively breathe in as a difficult trick is begun, letting out a large "oooooh" when it is completed. To this day I find myself taking an anticipatory breath when I see a child sassing a parent, because in my childhood this was always followed by a quick shot to a spot inducing temporary pain.

Stress

The nonverbal signs of stress are closely related to those of frustration, anger, and worry. Stress gestures often involve the fist: hands in fists at sides, crossed arms with fists, fists resting on a desk, banging the table with a fist. (The child's version is arm waving.) Clenched hands, a modified fist gesture, is also a sign of anxiety. Pictures of disaster survivors grieving for their lost friends or relatives frequently show the subjects in this position. It is almost as if we need to hang on to someone or something, even if it is ourselves in times of stress.

Another stress gesture is hand wringing. One TV advertisement for an office copier was designed to promote the portability of a particular model. The star of the ad talked to us as if we were in the office with him. He pointed out a feature of the copier and then turned away to explain it to us. Behind his back, someone rolled the copier off for other uses. When the actor turned back to the machine and realized it was missing, he made the typical hand-wringing gesture of anxiety. Turning back to the camera, he bumbled out of control until the person returned the machine.

We frequently show stress by rubbing the back of our neck, called *defensive beating*. A popular oil filter commercial features a smug service station mechanic pointing derisively at some poor yuk who is trudging to his car with an obviously large garage bill in hand. The mechanic says something like, "See this little thing? It costs about $5.00. He could have bought one of these and saved himself that big bill. You see, you can pay me now or you can pay me later." The effective part of the commercial is the actor in the background. He walks out to the car rubbing his neck like he's just pulled a muscle, looking at the bill and shaking his head. He gets in the car and just sits there, defensively beating himself until the commercial is over. A bartender reported to one researcher that the defensive-beating gesture was a good indicator of a potential fight. The fights were usually started by the defensive beater.

Many signs of worry or stress involve self-touching. A common one is rubbing the forehead, usually done with thumb on the cheekbone and the first and second finger on the forehead, as if rubbing away the worry lines. It also hints that we have a headache from all the problems. We often rub at our eyes, pull our cheeks, and generally rub our faces in a series of beaten exhaustion moves. We may even stretch slowly and rub parts of our body to psychologically wipe away the strain of the problem.

We also sigh a lot. Without the sigh, our daytime serial actors and actresses would be nearly mute.

(Sigh) "Lance, darling, I don't know what we're going to tell Larry about the results of the tests."

(Sigh) "Rachel, he must be told before Wanda gets to him about the affair."

(Sigh) "Wanda wouldn't do that, would she?"

"You know she's always hated us, Rachel."

(Sigh) "I guess we do deserve it, after testifying about her 'thing' for mint cookies at her incompetency trial."

The sigh says, "Listen to me, I have something more than air to get off my chest." It slows down the conversation; it gives dramatic pause. It gives us a chance to glaze over pained expressions and worried brows without the distraction of words. The sigh often says, "I'm under stress."

Skepticism

Closing off the center is a common indicator of skepticism, suspicion, or secretiveness. Arms crossed tightly over the chest or crossed casually on the desk signal a potential communications problem. Suspects being interrogated by the police frequently use their folded arms to help "clam up," closing their center (and mouth) as tight as a clam shell. A variation in a nonintimidating situation is to put one or both hands over your mouth, as if to say, "Speak no evil."

Scratching the face is another sign of skepticism. Comedian Bob Newhart started his career playing the skeptic in a number of unusual situations, such as being the watchman on the Empire State Building the night King Kong scaled it; being a game manufacturer the day Abner Doubleday called up to talk about baseball; and being a marketing adviser when inventor Herman Hollerith called to introduce his new punched-card sorter. Newhart's standard "You've got to be kidding" gesture is scratching underneath the eye with the middle finger. Some people also pinch the bridge of the nose, as if to say, "I don't believe this!"

We reject ideas by waving them away with a palm-out swipe from side to side as if to say, "Go on!" We use the hand in imitation of the head shake to say, "No, no, no" in a back-and-forth erasing motion. Psychologists theorize that the negative head shake is a relic from infancy when we nursed at the breast or bottle. When we were not hungry, we rejected the nipple by turning the head sharply to the side. Since I've never found a baby willing to talk about it (don't blame me, I've tried), I'm a bit skeptical of this interpretation. I believe that it is another cultural trait learned by imitation. For example, a parent wags a finger at a naughty child. Soon the child is wagging *his* finger at his dog or friends.

Nervousness

We have to move when we get too nervous. A theater audience begins to fidget when one of the characters is about to make a fool of himself. A co-worker tells us she just "can't sit still today." Something is moving all the time in nervous people. Their fingers drum the table, they tap their pencil, they doodle, or they tear paper into little pieces. I remember one customer who used to rub the stickum off transparent tape. (This is not an easy process, as any accomplished tape rubber will attest.)

Many men are terminal coin or key jinglers. I say terminal, because this irritates me so much that I'm tempted to kill them to stop the incessant noise. It's really the fault of pockets. I think the designers who developed the male suit actually hate men. The pockets are relatively useless. They form an unsightly bulge if filled with a handkerchief (especially if it is used), are impossible to get at if a man is sitting down, and are shaped so that the contents fall down to a narrow point that is only large enough for two fingers. With any normal luck, the pockets will wear out long before the suit so that they become a chute for discreetly depositing coins on the street or into a shoe. But since the pockets are there ("Why do I use my pockets? Because they are there."), men use them for miscellaneous possessions, usually metal.

The jingler is unaware of his actions, or else he surely would stop. Even ignoring the noise, it's an annoying nervous habit. I occasionally fall into it, too. To fight its effects, I keep my right pocket (I'm right-handed) empty of everything but my handkerchief. My coins and keys are in my left pocket. Since the pockets seem so irresistible, I have developed the habit of putting only my right hand in my pocket, which is also easier on the suits. Since there is nothing to play with other than a no-fun cloth, my hand stays fairly idle and my pocket-plunging needs are satisfied.

You can fight nervousness by keeping your mouth busy. Smoking is one way, if you're not too hung up about clogged lungs. Whistling is a healthier solution. Anna in *The King and I* found that whistling helped her fight nervousness and fear. Whistling, like yawning, seems to be a community affair. If one person in an office starts whistling, by lunchtime the whole organization sounds like a magpie convention during a spontaneous rally for their favorite bird.

We tend to do a lot of self-repair when we are nervous. Scientists call this *preening*, named after the action of birds who smooth their feathers. We tug at our skirt or pants. We brush at our hair with our hand or straighten our belt or tie. The more we do this and the longer it lasts, the more nervous we are. I have seen some job seekers preen through an entire 30-minute interview.

Self-Assurance and Superiority

One of the most condescending and irritating signs of self-assurance I have ever seen involved sports. When Red Auerbach was head coach of the Boston Celtics basketball team, he had a habit of lighting up a cigar when he felt victory was assured. The earlier he did this in the game, the more insulting he was to his opponent. The crowd and the announcers picked up on it and made it that much more noticeable. Nothing could have been more irritating to an opposing player than to see Auerbach smugly puffing his victory stogie.

The cigar often plays a triumphant role in business. At my old office, new fathers passed out congratulatory cigars. (Being a nonsmoker and a malcontent, I passed out candy. The hell with the men; it sure made the women happy.) Several managers who smoked cigars would light up occasionally after a particularly successful sales call or presentation. One of the engineers used to smoke a Friday afternoon "end of week celebration" cigar.

The cigar lost some of its macho image in our company one afternoon. I was talking to my manager in his office when the branch manager stomped in and shut the door. "Did you see what I saw?" he stormed. One of the new hires, a young woman 5'3" and all of 105 pounds, was nonchalantly smoking an inch-thick "New Baby" gift stogie with a group of salesmen.

My manager, who did most of the interviewing for the office and was more aware of what's fair these days, replied, "So what?"

"We can't have her in here smoking a cigar. What if one of the customers sees her or she does it at a customer location?"

"What are you going to do," my boss countered, "tell her she can't smoke cigars because she's a woman? The men can."

"I guess you're right, but it still bugs me. This would never have happened when *I* was a salesman. Sometimes I think we're going too far."

I can understand the branch manager's feelings at seeing another male symbol going by the wayside. What he didn't know is that it was already on its way out. The cigar has been losing some of its macho image ever since the dainty cigarette-sized cigars came out. "Should a gentleman offer an Armadillo to a lady?'' the ad queries. ''Not if he's a man!'' the branch manager might answer.

Placing the hands above the shoulders is another superiority gesture. Bruce Jenner threw fists up in victory as he crossed the finish line in the mile finale of the Olympic decathlon. The confident executive sitting in an office may lean back and talk with hands clasped behind his head. This gesture is always a part of a relaxed posture, which, as noted in Chapter 4, usually connotes higher status. The center is very open, almost aggressively open, with the hands in this position. Hands behind the head is primarily a male gesture. A woman who assumes this position will focus attention on her bust, a decided negative in a business situation.

Stretching is another example of the NVC restrictions women face in a male-oriented business world. In my classes all the students need to stretch after sitting for a long period of time. At a break, the men put their hands straight over their head, lean back in the chairs, swing their arms about, let out a grunt, and relax. Any woman who does the ''male'' version may appear to be provocative. The women go through all kinds of gymnastics to stretch without really stretching. All they are left with is a type of isometrics as they tense and relax their muscles without being able to let out a good stretch.

Putting our hands over our *head* is another sign of superiority. The boxer traditionally clenches his hands over his head. The President acknowledges the cheers of the crowd by waving both hands over his head. The football team chants, ''We're No. 1'' with hands up in the air, index fingers pointing to the sky. The Nazi salute was a typical superiority gesture.

Psychologists theorize that we raise our hands over our head to raise our height—that this series of gestures is tied to height might. This may be true, but many other self-assurance and superiority gestures don't require increased height. One of the most common is *steepling*. The typical steepling position is to have the hands with opposite fingertips touching (like a ''spider doing pushups on a mirror'') and fingers spread widely in the shape of a spired church. The elbows are usually on the table, so that the center is somewhat closed and the hands are up around the face. A less overbearing form of steepling is to clasp the hands in a prayer position, elbows on the table, with only the index fingers extended. Sometimes the chin rests on the thumbs and the index fingers are touching the lips.

The next level of steepling is to have the hands clasped with elbows on the table, possibly with the chin resting on the hands. Many businesspeople realize that none of these are good communications postures but unconsciously engage in modified steepling, laying their arms flat on the desk and grasping hands or sitting with hands clasped in their lap.

Hands on hips is another common self-assurance gesture. The Jolly Green Giant towers ominously over his valley standing with legs spread and hands on hips, booming his benevolent "Ho, ho, ho!" Mr. Clean gets rid of dirt and grime and grease in just a minute and, incidentally, stands around with hands on his hips. A mother will confront her child playing in the kitchen drawer with hands on hips, saying, "And what do you think *you're* doing?"

The strongest form of this gesture is to have the fists on the hips. The next strongest is to have the hands open and pointing downward, thumbs on one side of the hips and fingers on the other. Hands in pockets or thumbs looped into the top of pants or the belt loops are weaker versions.

Hands behind the back is a self-assurance gesture often used by leaders. The Army sergeant strides purposefully in front of the green recruits, chest thrust out, arms clasped behind his back. The teacher tells his students how poorly they have done on the midterm exam, hands clasped behind him as he shifts back and forth from the heels to the balls of his feet. (Again, this is not a common gesture for a woman, for the same reason mentioned in stretching.)

Insults and Anger

Consistent with human nature, our gesture vocabulary is full of insults. The most common is one mentioned earlier, the "finger" (or the "bird"), where the middle finger only is extended from the fist and displayed at our target. It is a very taunting gesture, suitable for someone who has just driven us off the road, heckled at our speech, insulted us, or made off with our date. It is being used more and more by both sexes. In the aftermath of the shootings at Kent State, National Guardsmen commented in surprise on the way the women students talked to them and how frequently this gesture was part of the conversation.

Next on the insult list is the gesture made by placing your left fist with palm down on your upper arm near the elbow and bringing the other arm up into a "shaking your fist" position. This says you can take an idea or comment and place it somewhere in the anatomy. The gesture is not nearly so eloquent as the finger, but it is more fun to do. If you need a more socially acceptable gesture, "thumbing your nose" has a certain poetry to it, as you put your thumb on your nose and waggle your fingers in derision. If noise is what you need, the Bronx cheer can show it with a wet "Blblblblbl" (just put your tongue between your lips and blow).

If it's disrespect you're looking for, flapping your ears could be the answer. In imitation of donkey ears, you put a thumb in each ear and wave your fingers. If you don't like to get your chin wet with the Bronx cheer, you can at least stick out your tongue. In a role-playing session recently with a large group of students, I played an argumentative employee and they took turns acting as my manager. When I backed one poor student into a corner and countered her last point, she crossed her arms in desperation, got a very determined look on her face, and stuck her tongue out at me. After the class and I recovered a few moments later, I teased her about breaking role and she replied, "Who broke role?"

We like to insult someone's intelligence by letting them know we think a "screw is loose" or there's "nobody home." The first we do by rotating the index finger near the temple; the second, by tapping the temple with the finger. We make the cuckoo sign (the brain is supposedly going round and round) by circling an index finger around our ear. Sometimes we roll our eyes and look skyward, as if to say, "Oh, Lord, why me?" A Xerox commercial that has run several seasons shows a monk who is told to make several hundred copies of an excruciatingly detailed handwritten manuscript. The enterprising monk sneaks off to his local copy center and comes back with copies the same day. When he presents them to his superior, who in awe mumbles, "It's a miracle!" the young monk rolls his eyes and looks off in disbelief at the superior's ignorance.

Another insulting gesture is the thumbs-down movement,

used to reject another person or idea. This gesture can be traced to ancient Rome, where it was used in audience surveys. When a gladiator was defeated in combat in the arena, the victor had the option of sparing him or killing him on the spot. The spectators could signal death by holding out their fists with the thumb pointing downward. Today we give the thumbs-down sign when someone else is talking and we want to indicate our disagreement without speaking. Thumbs down becomes an NVC "Kill it!" or "It'll never get off the ground, Orville."

As mentioned in Chapter 4, most gestures indicating anger are back-of-hand movements. Giving someone "the back of your hand" is one; shaking your fist is another. Finger pointing and chest poking can also indicate anger, although they are closely tied to frustration. You begin pointing a finger for emphasis in a conversation only when you feel that you aren't getting your point across or that the person is not listening. The more the person argues, the more violently you point.

Another indication of anger is not moving at all. You make no gestures as you talk or listen. This anger sign usually elicits the comment "Is there something wrong?" A teacher will stop talking and stand motionless until a whispering student notices that nothing else is going on in the room. A subordinate will sit rigidly still during the critical part of an appraisal as the boss details the subordinate's shortcomings for the year. Other versions of this are the "silent treatment" and the "cold shoulder." Our lack of NVC signs becomes a signal in itself!

Summary

You've had the chance to learn some of the standard gestures for showing emotions. Since many of these integrate several parts of the body, they were examined in what researchers call "gesture clusters." In the next chapter you will learn NVC behavior clusters for a variety of common business situations. By understanding your environment and making maximum use of NVC in these situations, you can increase your ability to communicate successfully in the business world.

6

NVC in the Office

There are a number of common business situations where you can exercise your new knowledge of NVC. Some, like riding in an elevator, are merely fun to experiment with. Others, like meeting someone in an interview, can help you communicate better.

The Elevator Syndrome

It never ceases to amaze me that the most dynamic people in the world become shy and awkward on the elevator. Riding an elevator has to be one of the most uncomfortable events of our day. Because of this, there is a complete set of unwritten rules in elevator behavior. When you walk in, you punch the proper button, move to the nearest open spot, and turn to face the front. All conversation must stop. As more people get in, you shuffle over (nobody ever *walks* or takes steps inside an elevator) to make room, preferably not touching anyone. If you must touch someone, you keep your body stiff and unmoving at all times as if to say, "Uh, I'm not getting any pleasure out of touching you." As the elevator empties, you again shuffle so there are even spaces between you and the other occupants. If you are in back and need to get out, you mumble, "Out, please" or "'Scuse me" deferentially. At no time do you look anywhere but at the lighted numbers above the door or at the top of the button panel.

I can see the UFO training instructor getting ready for a close encounter of the third kind:

"Today class, we are going to study the archaic human up-and-down box. Now remember, the first rule is *no gronkling*."

A slow student pipes up innocently, "But don't these poor beasts wish to share their discomfort by communicating with each other in their little box?"

"I can see you still don't understand the primitive human animal, Thyroid. It's true that humans crowd themselves into little buglike transportation devices for amusement, pack themselves into a dark room to watch projected images, or attend a sports contest and scream with thousands of their own kind. But they really don't like to be together. It makes little sense, I know, but that's what you've got to keep in mind if you want to pass."

Poor Thyroid didn't realize that the elevator is really an NVC nightmare. All those strangers are shoved into intimate spaces. Sometimes they even are forced to *touch*. (I always seem to end up behind the lady with the beehive or the Afro.) There is no place to morally rest their gaze. And since they are together for such a short time, they have no chance to transform themselves from nonpeople to real people.

There are a number of different approaches to this discomfort. Some people walk on and stand right in front of the button panel. They are out of the way of the door with their backs to a wall where they won't be forced to move as the car fills and empties. Though everyone entering the car has to reach around them to punch a floor button, they maintain the "panel position." Others go straight to the back of the elevator and lean against the rail, even if they are getting off at the next floor. Still others prefer to travel the elevator in pairs, much like women in a restaurant going to the bathroom in tandem. They wait until someone else they know is elevator-bound and then walk on together. Their conversation dies as they enter and restarts in mid-sentence as they depart. What all these people would really like to do is to walk straight to the back of the car, stand facing the wall about six inches away, and over their shoulder say, "Somebody tell me when we get to the fifteenth floor."

You can experiment with your new knowledge of NVC the

next time you ride an elevator. Pick a spot somewhat off to the side (but away from the walls) and don't move as the car fills and empties. This will throw everyone's territorial space gyrations out of kilter. If you end up on the same side with the only other occupant, see how he or she reacts. If you have the fortitude, get on a crowded elevator, push your button, then face the crowd, looking everyone in the eyes. Most of us hate people who do this, so don't get carried away. One executive likes to get on the elevator, face the crowd saying, "You may wonder why I called this meeting," and then turn around. Try it.

Another behavior that makes us uncomfortable in an elevator is loud talking. Mustering your courage one day, get on your elevator and boom to the crowd, "Howya all doin' today? Nice weather we're having, isn't it? How many came in on Highway 40 today?" When nothing happens, say, "C'mon, let's see a show of hands." If you still get no response, start asking them one by one, "Do you drive to work?" This is really fun in the morning when everybody is grumpy and half-awake anyway.

I had an opportunity to experiment with elevator NVC when I was a salesman. My company was located on floors 8, 9, and 10 of our 15-story building. Employees were always going a short hop up or down while the other building tenants were going the full trip to or from the lobby. Another salesman named Jim and I started a quick-thinking creativity game involving weird stories. If I was riding up to 10 from the lobby and Jim got on at 8, the conversation would go something like this:

"Jim! When did they let you out of jail?"

"Oh, the lawyer posted bail in about two hours," Jim would reply, quickly picking up the game.

"Did they ever find the gun?"

"No, but her family is still out looking for it with the police. If they find it, no telling what will happen . . . "

We'd walk off at 10 leaving a carful of people leaning after us as the doors swished closed. The game, of course, was to throw an outrageous opening line at the other person and see who would get stumped or break up first. I like to think we brightened the lives of many of our fellow travelers. (The idea for this wasn't original with us, though. We thought of it when we followed two secretaries all the way to 14 listening to them talk about their dates that weekend. I never did find out what the blonde did after her date stopped the car.)

Greeting Behavior

Part of the problem in an elevator is that we don't have the time to properly greet one another. We've probably all ridden the elevator hundreds of times with people who work on nearby floors without ever meeting or greeting them. The first stage of a true greeting is *orientation.* I once was walking down the hall at one of my major customer's offices when I passed a man who looked very familiar. I must have looked familiar to him too, because we both had a puzzled look on our faces as we passed. We had noticed each other and were in that uncertain area where you don't know whether to say hello and risk feeling foolish or to ignore the other person and risk being insulting. When we were about 15 feet past each other, we both turned simultaneously to look back. When he exclaimed, "Ken!" his name came to me. It was a personnel executive I had talked to six months earlier about putting on a seminar for his division. We laughed about acting in unison in our mutual confusion. We had both noticed each other but had been trapped in indecision over whether we should greet.

When the executive turned, I saw the second stage of greeting: the *eyebrow flash.* After you orient your eyes to someone, your eyebrows move sharply upward. If there is a delay in recognition, there will be a double flash as your eyebrows first move up in recognition, then move higher in greeting. I'm the type of person who likes to sit in hotel lobbies and flash my eyebrows in recognition and greeting at passers-by. That sign alone is enough to make people stop and come over to talk, or at least wave as they continue on.

The third stage of greeting is the *salutation.* It is always a good idea to include a person's name in your salutation. Repeating the name helps you remember it the next time you meet. It is also music to your friend's ears. We all love to hear our name. You can hardly say it too much. Have you ever gone up to someone you thought you knew from behind, tapped her on the shoulder, and said, "Hi, Sally!" only to have her turn around and be someone else? As you slink away looking like a mobile red stoplight, you vow never to make that mistake again. You can take advantage of name sensitivity to avoid such cases of mistaken identity. Go up behind the person and quietly say his or her name. If you get any reaction out of your target, you know you have the right person and can continue in safety.

The fourth stage of greeting is *presenting the palm*. We can do this with a wave. A man will usually wave his whole hand at the wrist by rotating his forearm. A woman will wave by holding her hand up and bending only the fingers or by moving the fingers independently in a ripple motion. If you are close enough for contact, the acceptable business greeting is the handshake. The hand extension for the shake should be well timed. I have seen two men do the "quick-draw boogie" as one put his hand out too early and withdrew it when the other person extended his hand. The longer your hand is extended ungrasped, the greater your embarrassment and insult.

Your handshake is a large part of the first impression you create. Pity the people with cold or naturally sweaty hands, for they have a strike against them. (Breathing on your hand or wiping your hand on your pants or skirt before you shake only makes matters worse.) When I was a salesman, I always wore a warm pair of gloves so my hands didn't feel like ice cubes when I greeted another person. I also made it a habit of keeping my right hand out of my pocket and carrying my leather attaché case in my left hand to avoid a sweaty handshake. If I had to dry my hand, I tried to do it unobtrusively a few minutes before the end of the discussion.

The pressure of a handshake is also important. We've all shaken hands with the "dead fish" and wanted to buy back our introduction. One of the engineers in my office had this type of handshake. Although he was a strong, beefy guy, his handshake was wet toast. When I mentioned it to him, he explained that he had accidentally injured some people when shaking hands. A good "rule of thumb" is to match the pressure used by the person you are shaking hands with.

The politician's handshake, offering the hand in an L shape so only the fingers can be grasped, is poor in business. You should always offer your full hand to someone, unless you are meeting a macho limb crusher. If a crusher gets your knuckles in his grip, you are maimed. The best approach is to thrust your hand fully into his so that your knuckles are past his grip and hope for an early parole.

The last stage of proper greeting is *eye contact*. Most of us have been taught to maintain strong eye contact as we meet—to look another person in the eye and not back down until we are seated and into our conversation. Wrong! When you meet people, especially for the first time, always give them a few seconds to look at you unobserved so they can form that necessary first impression. For example, when a man interviews a woman for a job, he wants to check out what he sees initially (legs, hair, and so on) and then give the woman the once-over, unobserved. While women may not like it, this seems to be a fact of business life. If a man doesn't get the opportunity, he will try to sneak looks during the conversation. This distracts him, at best, from the real job of interviewing. The same is often true with a man being interviewed. I've asked executives what they look for first in a male candidate. While there is no consensus, the most frequently named items are hair length, clothing, pants crease, and shoeshine. Until an executive judges those, he will not be completely relaxed.

You should provide each person you meet with two or three seconds of unobserved eye contact directly after the handshake. In my sales calls, I always did this deliberately. I would look away, turn to put my coat down, lay my briefcase out, take the chair facing the person, sit down, grab whatever papers I needed, and finally look up. Although this took only a few seconds, it gave my customer enough time to observe me in privacy. I once experimented with skipping this part of the greeting, but the potential cost in lost sales was too great for me to continue. My success rate in first-time calls was measurably higher with this pause.

We have another intricate set of procedures for greeting people at distances. When we see a friend coming toward us on the street or down a long office corridor, we quickly look down and keep walking until the person is about ten feet away. As if on cue, we look up in unison, exchange greetings, and then look back down as we pass. (It always amazes me when I see high-level executives walking with their eyes at their feet.) We have to look down because the other person is too far away for us to look at as we approach without extending into immoral looking time.

Just for fun, the next time you are walking along and see acquaintances down the hall coming at you, look at them and greet them the entire time. Keep smiling and waving as you approach; it will drive them crazy. They'll be a basket of potatoes by the time you meet. If you want to bother people, do just the opposite. Keep looking down until you are abreast and then quickly look up as they pass and say hello. You'll be by them and heading away before they have a chance to respond. They are left thinking, "Should I say hello to him?" or "Will she think I snubbed her?"

There are other times when we wish to pass through a group without any contact. Sociologists call this *territorial passage*. The most obvious sign that people want to avoid communication is lack of eye contact. They will pass through the group with their eyes down, mumbling, "Excuse me" or "Pardon me." (I'm sorry I can't pardon you; you'll have to ask the governor.) Their hands will frequently be held down or in front of the body, further showing their desire to pass unnoticed. If someone wishes to join the group, he or she will attempt to move into the circle of discussion. If the group expands and the members open up their centers, the newcomer will maintain heavy eye contact with the speaker and group members and eventually take a verbal "turn."

Conversation

Taking a verbal turn isn't always as easy as it sounds. We have all been in a situation where we "couldn't get a word in edgewise." Worse yet, we've been trapped in a conversation, forced to sit there nodding our head like one of those annoying little dolls in the rear window of an automobile. A student told of being at a gathering with a woman who was a tipsy nonstop talker. Being polite, the student wasted nearly two hours trying to get away from this marathon mouth.

Other people have a habit of interrupting frequently. One of the hardest lessons for a sales trainee is learning when the customer is finished talking. I had one particularly slow-moving (and slow-thinking) customer who would insert long, reflective pauses into our conversations. At first, I assumed he was done and immediately responded to his comments. He would patiently wait for me to finish and then continue where he left off, ignoring everything I had said. This customer still holds my world's record for the longest pause in the middle of a conversation: 60 seconds. Yes, he once sat for a full minute before continuing with his next sentence. In crowds, he is relatively quiet because no one is willing to wait that long for the next thought to drop.

It's simple to determine when someone is done talking. We tend to mark the end of our speeches with physical signals. We look down or away when we are done, breaking eye contact and control of the conversation. Many times a change in posture will accompany the change in speakers. On a recent vacation to the Bahamas I saw good examples of this in the hotel lobby. The tours operating from the hotel required the guests to be out of their rooms by noon on the day of departure. Since the planes did not leave until five in the evening, the lobby was full of guests killing time. Almost as if they had all read the same book, the individual conversations were carefully marked. As one man stopped talking, settling back as he looked away, his companion would lean forward to begin talking. As she finished, she would turn slightly and cross her legs for her listening stint.

When people are not done talking, they will hold their postural position. They will not look down or away and down. They will keep their head and hands up to show a desire to continue. If they are in a group, they may use sounds to maintain control of the conversation. Sounds like "er," "uh," and "ah" keep people talking and force others to appear to be interrupting. Another way to "hold the floor" is to look up and away during pauses. I always joke that there must be a pornographic picture of a man and woman at the point where the wall and ceiling meet in every room because people look there so much. If you want to make a dramatic, reflective pause in your conversation without being interrupted, the wall–ceiling glance is your best bet. Accompanied by a little thoughtful chin rubbing, it will turn you into a surefire intellectual.

Listeners will signal when they want to make a comment to take over the conversation, usually by assuming an erect readiness posture and giving a fast series of agreement nods. Figure 6–1 shows a manager with his secretary. In the top picture, the manager is talking; in the bottom picture, the secretary is responding. Notice that when the manager is speaking he sits as close to the desk as possible and leans forward. He has a slight smile on his face and is palming with one hand. His other hand rests relaxed on the desk. He appears to have a very careful, controlled nature. His coat is still on, and the papers on his desk are neatly arranged in rows. He's obviously a right-hander, with his coffee cup, phone, and pens all lying to his right. The office is in the normal back-to-wall arrangement. The secretary is sitting in a relaxed, slightly slumping posture. Her arms are crossed in a modified closed center and her legs are crossed casually.

In the lower picture, where the secretary is speaking, several changes have taken place. She has uncrossed her legs and arms, moved up in the chair, and assumed an upright posture. One leg is tucked under her chair in a readiness or alertness position. Her chin is tilted up. The manager has assumed an open listening position. His arms are resting comfortably on his chair. He has pushed away from the desk and is leaning back in a superiority posture. His chin has dropped, indicating that he has stopped speaking, but he has not brought his head into a submissive position. His head remains level, a very open sign.

In your conversations, watch for the NVC signs that act as traffic signals for the discussion. If you don't see a marker such as a postural shift, dropped head, or eye contact, be quiet. Your partner will signal you when he or she is finished.

There are a number of NVC signs that indicate whether you are really getting through when you talk. In a good conversation, both parties will often assume the same body position. One salesman in my office did this so often in the casual bull sessions on the sales floor that I couldn't resist trying a small experiment. We

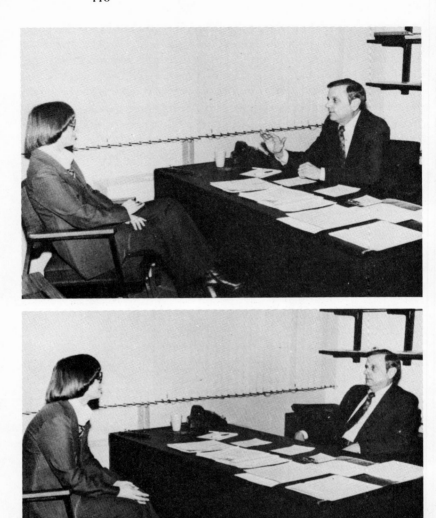

Figure 6–1. Conversation body positions.

started talking at my desk, which was next to a window. When I sat on my desk, he sat on the desk too. I casually moved over to the window and he followed, keeping his normal personal space. I sat on the heater module, tucking one leg under me, and he did the same. I stood up, and within one or two sentences he stood up. I finally put my foot up on the heater module, which was about desk high. He was quite a bit shorter than I am, but he pulled up his pants leg, put his foot on the module, and stood there straining to keep his balance until I felt guilty and moved back to my desk.

While this case is extreme, it does indicate how we signal a deep level of communication by mirroring the body positions of those we are speaking to. Another good indicator of successful conversation is *resonance*. We all tend to move synchronously with someone we are listening to. When the top picture in Figure 6–1 was taken, the secretary was bobbing her crossed leg in time to the boss's right-handed gesture. Sometimes we nod our head in time to a speaker's movements, as if to say, "I agree" or "I understand." We may drum our fingers in time to the pacing of an instructor or sway to the music of a film presentation.

Resonance is also an indicator of relative status. Whoever controls the tempo of the movements is usually the higher-status person, or the NVC leader. If you notice yourself resonating with someone else, change the tempo and see if the other person follows. If you observe two people resonating in a conversation, watch who begins a pattern and who follows, then see if that agrees with their status relationship.

Instructing and Presenting

Instructing or making presentations is a special type of conversation. People who treat instruction as a one-way communications process are making the mistake of communicating "to" instead of "with" their audience. Sometimes people end up communicating the wrong information, which can detract from their real message.

I once ran into this problem in one of my seminars for

women. Midway through the morning, the woman sitting in the front row farthest to my left began to giggle. Fearing the worst, I paused and asked her what she knew that I didn't. She managed to choke out, "You have a safety pin in the seat of your trousers."

I knew at once what had happened. In a class the previous week, I had accidentally sat down on a piece of fluorescent pink chalk. When my wife took the pants to the cleaners, they had evidently put a safety pin on the stain. There are certain things you can't do and be cool, and patting your rear in search of a safety pin in front of 25 women is one of them.

I made a similar gaffe recently just before I was to give an early morning body language speech to a large group of computer salespeople. The meeting was held locally, so I merely had to rise early and drive to the hotel across town. But being a true night person, I felt like a 45 rpm record being played at $33\frac{1}{3}$ on the way over. After asking only three people how to find the headquarters room, I walked in to meet my contact. He introduced me to all the people in the room—two women and four men—and then took me to his boss. I remember thinking they were a particularly friendly and cheerful bunch for such an early time of the day, a nice group. My contact suddenly got a strange look on his face and then asked, "Would you like to go to the cafeteria for a cup of coffee?"

Not sensing the urgency in his voice, I replied, "No thanks, I'm not a coffee drinker."

His boss broke in and said, "Then why don't we walk on over and take a look at the auditorium where you'll be speaking? I'm sure you want to get comfortable with the facilities." As we walked over, he quietly said, "Your fly is down."

Now every man has been caught by this joke dozens of times in his life. The secret is not to panic and clutch at your crotch. To be on the safe side, I said, laughing, "This is why I carry a briefcase," and held my leather folio in front of my waist. I took a few more steps thinking, "Why would he pull this one on me?" As I brushed my fingers over the top of my zipper, I noticed a distinct separation. (That jaunt in from the car *had* seemed kind of cold.) I had just walked through a crowded lobby and met some members of my meeting group, fly flapping and white jockey shorts winking brightly through the gap. Thank goodness I hadn't worn my paisley bikini undershorts. (I save those for important occasions.)

Trying to salvage some measure of self-respect after being the body language expert who showed up opened up, I mentioned the old flying joke, "Well, my brother the pilot told me you should never fly if you're the type of pilot who walks out of the bathroom with your zipper down." When that was rewarded with a sincere chuckle, I thanked the boss, "Charlie, I appreciate your not letting me go up there like this. Of course, they would always have wondered if I did it on purpose and I would never have told them."

Appearance is critical in any group communications session. Think of either of these two stories before you rush into a meeting. No matter how late you are, there is always time for a quick 360-degree turn in front of a mirror to spot any irregularities that will destroy your image and change initial respect into derision.

GOOD PRESENTATION NVC

Chapter 2 discussed the importance of laying out a room to give an audience comfortable personal space. One of the problems with many presentations is that there is too much space between the presenter and the audience. In a small conference room holding 20 to 25 people, the lectern may be as far as 15 feet from the first row of chairs. If the attendees, like most people, tend to be "balcony Baptists," the space is even greater.

I always move the lectern up whenever possible. When I can work without notes, I stand as close as possible to the audience without invading the social territorial space of the people in front. This has several advantages. First, the audience is easier to control at closer range. The farther away you are, the easier it is for an audience to whisper, doodle, or doze off. The increased distance gives them a false sense of invisibility. Height advantage is also diminished with distance. If there is an interruption, it is much more difficult to regain your listeners' attention if they are 15 feet away. Finally, your voice may not be able to reach the rear rows of listeners. It is not enough to be heard by those in back; you must be heard throughout your full *range* of speaking to be effective.

It is often helpful to actually "get into" your group during a presentation. During an advanced business seminar that I attended at Harvard Business School one of the professors used this technique. He literally ran up and down the aisles getting to people who wanted to make a comment or ask a question. Although the students were initially amused by the professor's antics, they paid more attention to him than to any other speaker in the course. The class was also much more informal and relaxed.

You can create a more relaxed atmosphere by keeping your center open. I never say a word to a formal group with my coat buttoned, nor do I ever wear a vest to a talk or presentation. Whenever possible, I remove my coat. I do not loosen my tie in a business setting, because I believe it looks sloppy. The loose-tie image is better for after 5:00 P.M. when you are trying to convince your boss that you're working too hard. I believe this informality does not apply as strongly to women. A woman should appear competent and professional to overcome the possible prejudices of the audience. This is hard to achieve if a woman gives a presentation in a relaxed, open manner. A woman can make her presentation more personable through voice and delivery.

A problem that speakers of both sexes have is eye contact. As mentioned in Chapter 4, people normally maintain eye contact less than 50 percent of the time when speaking. In addressing a group, the presenter must break this rule dramatically, maintaining eye contact with *somebody* nearly 100 percent of the time. This total eye contact can be extremely uncomfortable. Many instructors try to solve the problem by looking only at one student, seeing the audience as a sea of impersonal faces or not looking at the audience at all. Some presenters pick a spot slightly above everyone's head in the back of the room and watch it as they talk. This gives the same distracted effect as a TV personality reading teleprompted lines just off camera.

You must develop an "audience scan" technique. The goal is to make all the members of the group feel as if you have looked at them personally during the talk. If you let your eyes sweep across the audience, you are not really making any eye contact. Your gaze must jump from person to person, resting on each one for at least "moral looking time." Anything less is ineffective; anything more is intimidating. You have to be doubly conscious of the edges of the group—front, back, left and right. If your eye jumps in a left-to-right, up-and-back pattern, you will be looking at the edges only half as much as the middle. This is particularly true of the front corners.

I find that simply scanning randomly and concentrating on hitting the edges more often is sufficient to help me maintain better eye contact. I don't follow a specific pattern because I'm afraid to look like a searchlight flashing regularly in the night. This random pattern works effectively for very large groups too, because you can hit more people with a single jump. At a distance of 50 feet, 15 or 20 people will all think you are looking at them individually.

At times you may want to intimidate an unruly listener. A silent, piercing gaze will direct the group's attention to the offender. We've all been talking to someone during a meeting and suddenly noticed that the room was quiet with everyone looking at us. I've always been tempted to scream, clutch my heart, and fall to the ground when this happened to me. (This would be a lot of fun and is a great way to change jobs.)

There is also a rule about gestures in presenting: make some. Many speakers cling to the lectern like a liferaft. If the speaker ever lets go, he or she will drown. The presenter starts with both hands gripping the sides of the lectern. As the speaker moves to the left, the right hand lets go and grabs the left side before the left hand lets go. The process is reversed in moving to the right. Occasionally, the speaker may daringly let go and make a feeble move with one hand before vertigo sets in and the errant hand returns to its permanent roost.

In addition to making gestures, unlock yourself from the lectern. I've found that my listeners are much more responsive when they have a moving target to follow. If you stand in one place, you will lull your listeners into a stupor, similar to highway-stripe hypnosis. Their eyes need to move around in their heads, and their heads need to swivel to keep the brain lubricated. This doesn't mean you have to put on roller skates every time you plan to stand up and say something; but the longer you talk, the more you should provide your audience with a variety of movements for visual stimulation.

When you must stand at the lectern, don't fall into the "Coast Guard sway" shown in Figure 6–2. This is when you tightly grip the lectern on both sides, feet planted widely, and sway left and right toward the side walls as you speak. You had better put Dramamine into the coffee, because the only listeners who won't be seasick in a few minutes are the Coast Guard people. Interact *with* rather than *along* your audience by placing your feet approximately shoulder width apart and putting one foot slightly in front of the other (your "best foot" forward of course). No side-to-side movement is possible in this position. Instead, it will allow you to shift toward the group for emphasis and away from it for reflection. Imagine an old-time preacher leaning low over the lectern and shouting, "You're all going to

Figure 6–2. Lectern stance.

hell!'' He leans back suddenly upright and softly asks, ''What do you think about that?''

These skills can help you make better presentations. You also need to know when you are succeeding and when you are losing in the competition for your audience's attention. I can always tell who hasn't done the homework in my college classes. A student may walk in and claim, ''I really liked that Principles of Management book. Yep, I read the first eight chapters and it was *so* engrossing.'' When I glance down at the student's desk, I notice that the book sits there without a binding gap from being opened. Then when I ask for volunteers to discuss the chapters, the student goes on an eye contact vacation.

One of the sure signs of a lost audience is when you can't find a volunteer. You are suddenly so alone that you may as well take off your clothes. People look down at their papers, pick at their nails, or gaze abstractly into space. I like to just stand there until someone can't take it any more and looks up out of curiosity. I then have my subject, and make a mental note to figure out what I'm doing wrong.

I also like to make a game of calling on students who have questions before they raise their hand. The NVC signals for ''wanting to speak'' are about 80 percent reliable (though occasionally I've recognized people who are just about to scratch their heads). As in conversation, listeners who want to add to the discussion will usually change positions, sitting alertly as if to say, ''I intend to speak when there is a gap.'' They will also maintain solid eye contact with the presenter in order to attract attention when their turn arrives. Another tipoff is that they will make some kind of noise, such as clearing their throat or saying ''er,'' to verbally get in line behind the current speaker.

Listeners will also signal attentiveness. As noted earlier attentiveness is determined in part by where people sit in a room (see Zones of Attention in Chapter 2). But body position is a much stronger indicator. The King Kong head tilt is a very positive sign of attention, as is resonance with the speaker's movements. Hand-to-side-of-face gestures also show evaluation. Examples of these are forefinger on cheek with thumb and second finger on chin, fingers on cheek, fingers stroking chin, or head on fist. We also sometimes fondle objects such as a pipe or glasses in order to buy time to make an evaluation.

Figure 6–3 shows part of a class that has been kept too late. There is only one positive NVC sign among the three students: the woman's evaluative right-hand position. This is negated by her posture. Like the two men, she is leaning away from the instructor. None of the students' centers is particularly open to the speaker, and two are closed off with either hands or crossed legs. All three have very sober, set facial expressions. The man on the left has a level head position with face turned toward the speaker. The woman also has a normal head position, but her head is turned slightly away from the direction of her gaze. The man on the right has a very negative dominant-disagree head position to go with his closed center and leaning posture. Both men are also gesturing with modified steepling (superiority). This is clearly a negative group of students who are showing little empathy or agreement with their instructor.

Figure 6–3. Losing an audience.

Gestures of boredom or impatience are another sign of losing your audience. I always joke that the best NVC sign that an instructor is "burying" a class is a red spot on a student's forehead after a break. (The red spot is from resting face down on the table.) A shaking or tapping foot is also a consistent indicator of uninvolvement. Drumming fingers, twiddling thumbs, and doodling are other signals. The head-in-hand gesture (not to be confused with hand to side of face) is the worst. If the chin is resting in the open palm with the fingers splayed over one cheek, you can be certain the eyelids will begin to flutter soon after.

As much as I hate to see signs of inattention, they have been of great use to me in teaching. I have very little desire to talk to sleeping people. No matter what my schedule, I'm better off blowing it with several extra breaks than mesmerizing my students in a frantic marathon day. In communicating with an audience, you too should make it easier for people to listen to you and you should "listen" with your eyes for their attentiveness.

Offices and Meeting Rooms

OFFICE LAYOUTS

As mentioned in Chapter 2, an office is an excellent indicator of its owner's personality. Figure 6–4 shows three views of one of the most unusual offices I have ever seen. The top photograph shows the view from the door, the middle photograph shows the view from the plant, and the bottom photograph shows the view from the visitor's chair. This is one of those rare offices with the occupant's back to the door. The executive likes this arrangement because he is "not distracted by people walking past outside the door." Still, it takes a very confident and self-assured personality to ignore rear fear. It also takes a lot of self-discipline not to become distracted by sounds outside the door.

The office is highly individualized. Classical music plays softly in the background. The thriving greenery is not the result of a secretary's zealousness; it has been nurtured with protective concern by the executive himself. The major wall decoration is a *New Yorker* map of the United States, showing all points west of

Figure 6–4. An unusual executive office.

New York City as something akin to the Indian territories. A clock is mounted in prominent view. The shelves display a variety of cards, mementos, and books on many subjects.

The desk is efficiently arranged. In the middle picture, notice the piles of paper in convenient stacks. Necessary tools such as a stapler and staple remover are out on the desk. The pens are neatly laid out directly in front of the executive (to the left of his glasses). The executive appears organized but extremely busy. Compare this picture with the office in Figure 6–1. That executive's desk is much less cluttered and much more organized. No utensils are out; no personal effects show except for the nameplate in the front left corner. The shelves and credenza contain only pertinent books and folders. This office is much more impersonal, giving a serious, "no frills" approach to business.

Figure 6–5 is a diagram of the office pictured in Figure 6–4. It indicates several interesting features in addition to the occupant's chair facing away from the door. First, the office is designed to

Figure 6–5. Office layout.

minimize a visitor's stay if the occupant desires. The executive has a small office space to work with and evidently wishes to control most of it. The visitor has very little space, being hemmed in by the plant, desk, couch, and end table. As the bottom picture in Figure 6–4 shows, the plant can get in the way of a conversation across the desk. As in the service station commercial, the plant and the visitor "can be *very* friendly."

Although the visitor does not have enough space to feel totally comfortable, the chair is tall enough (and the executive's chair unmodified) so that the visitor is not at a height disadvantage. In fact, the executive will often put himself at a height disadvantage by sitting on the couch to talk to a visitor. In addition to relaxing his guest, this move opens the centers by removing the desk as an obstruction and minimizes the plant's interference. The location of the couch and the executive's willingness to sit "one down" further emphasize his confidence and self-assurance.

FORMAL MEETINGS

I recently examined a government agency conference room with a carefully designed arrangement. The diagram in Figure 6–6 gives the basic features. In this highly structured organization, the seating layout is the basic King Arthur arrangement. At one end of the wide table, the commanding general sits flanked by his chief of staff and deputy. The agency directors sit along the sides in predetermined positions. The greater the director's seniority, the closer he sits to the general. Other meeting attendees sit behind the general in six or seven rows of chairs, with special support staff for a particular meeting sitting in the front row. The closer staff members are to the front row, the higher their status.

Those not seated at the table make their presentations at the lecterns. The left lectern is used if there is only one briefer; both are used if two are speaking. The screen is rear projection, so no audiovisual paraphernalia is exposed. The lighting is uniform, and the heavy drapes over the windows are never opened. The fire door behind the left lectern is always locked from the outside. The main door is behind the rows of chairs, an appropriate distance away from the general's seat to minimize rear fear.

Figure 6–6. Government agency conference room.

INFORMAL MEETINGS

Although we may occasionally attend rigidly structured meetings such as those held in a government agency, we can use NVC to better advantage in more informal meetings. When I was a computer salesman, I discovered quite a lot about one of my customers through a series of informal meetings. The customer had ordered a large computer system upgrade and was having trouble planning and coordinating the physical installation. One of the executives suggested that those involved on both sides begin meeting weekly until the installation was completed. I was the marketing representative for my company and was accompanied by two systems engineers, a hardware maintenance engineer, and a programming maintenance engineer. The customer's representatives included the programming supervisor, the operations manager, and an operations supervisor. I was responsible for leading and coordinating my company's efforts, but the customer had no single person in charge. In addition, no one had been designated to lead the meeting itself.

When I arrived at the conference room about 15 minutes before the first meeting, I found the customer's programming supervisor already seated at the head of the table, facing the door. It was apparent that he intended to run the meeting. I was content to let that happen and decided to mill around until the meeting started and observe how everyone else reacted. The conference room was long and narrow, with two tables arranged end to end the length of the room. Approximately ten people could sit on each side. As people filed in, they glanced about the room and, seeing the programming supervisor at the far end, sat down at the other end near the door. I chose a chair in the middle of the group and sat down, fighting a smile. My hunch was that the programming supervisor was very defensive and was probably isolated from the others because he was not well liked.

The seating arrangement was almost comical. There were at least five empty seats between the supervisor and any other person at the meeting. One of the systems engineers walked in late and, looking around in puzzlement, picked a seat midway between the group and the supervisor ("out of sympathy," as he later told me). The funniest moment was when the supervisor began the meeting by saying, "You know, you don't all have to sit down there. I feel all alone." The participants looked at each other expectantly and shifted in their chairs, like the contestants on *To Tell the Truth* before the *real* person stands up. But they all stayed seated. After an embarrassed silence, the supervisor began the meeting.

As the weeks wore on, I found that my guess about the supervisor and his relationships had been correct. He was not well liked, and people were resentful of his leadership, even though he was the logical person to run the meeting. He sensed the resentment and bolstered his security by sitting with his back to the wall. The attendees retaliated by keeping their distance. The incredible thing was that we sat like this every week for three months. After the first few meetings, people became accustomed to the arrangement and found their ritual locations.

The lessons to me were clear. Whenever I gave a presentation at the customer's location or wanted to control or lead any type of meeting, I arrived early and claimed the end seat *nearest the door*. This let the other attendees sit with their backs to the wall. I also pulled chairs at the other end of the room away from the table and pushed them against the wall. I then spaced out the remaining chairs along the table, leaving no chairs at the far end. This forced the attendees to sit closer to me. I learned never to have more chairs at a conference table than I thought I would need, because people will use the ones that give them the most uninfringed territorial space.

Figure 6–7 is a diagram of another meeting where seating position was important. The meeting was called to market an advanced computer system to appropriate data processing personnel and the potential users of the system. I brought two experts in from out of town along with my systems engineer. The experts sat down first, across from each other at the middle of the table. The first customer to arrive and sit down was the data processing manager. I sat across from him. Although the programming supervisor and the users worked in different parts of the building, they arrived together and picked the positions shown. The systems engineer then sat next to the supervisor. This seating arrangement gave me all the information I needed to plan my sales strategy for the meeting.

On the basis of what you have read thus far, you should be able to answer the following questions:

1. What was the relationship between the manager and his subordinate, the programming supervisor?
2. What was the relationship between the users and the supervisor? The users and the manager?
3. What role did the manager and I intend to play in the meeting?
4. What role did the systems engineer plan to play?
5. How did the users feel about the proposal?

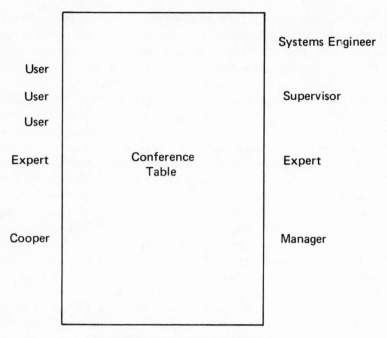

Figure 6–7. Informal meeting.

It was evident that there was no love lost between the programming supervisor and his manager. The supervisor waited until the manager was seated and then chose the one location where it would be almost impossible for him to converse with (or even see) the manager. The three users hovered uncertainly until the supervisor sat down and then sat across from him for easy conversation.

I had no intention of doing anything more than introducing the participants and letting the experts talk to the users. The manager evidently felt the same way, because he too picked a location with little dominance. I later found out he was there just to monitor the meeting and put a stop to any user interest in the marketing presentation. My systems engineer had been working closely with the supervisor and wanted to help him, but he also wanted to get to know the users better. The users were obviously interested enough to come to the meeting, but they were extremely defensive, particularly toward the manager. They made no effort to interact with the manager, although he was primarily responsible for any projects affecting them. And at no time before, during, or after the meeting did any one user ever get as far as ten feet from the other two.

My systems engineer had chosen his seat correctly. If the users were to be influenced, it would have to be through the supervisor, not his boss. I directed the conversation as much as possible to the opposite end of the table, as the systems engineer soon caught on to my strategy and took over. Afterward, I made it a point to engage the users in a technical conversation until long after the manager had a reason to remain. When he left, I scheduled a follow-up session for the discussions. The two experts were directed to a cab out front, content that they had done their job and oblivious to the wealth of information the meeting had revealed.

It pays to watch how participants mill around before a meeting starts. Figure 6–8 shows a small group talking before an informal departmental meeting. The woman and man on the left are supervisory personnel. Their manager is to the far right, and one of his secretaries is shown from the rear. Notice how both men have modified-aggressive NVC signs; the women are much less aggressive. The supervisor in the vest is standing with center open, head confidently cocked looking down from a height advantage, one hand in his pocket, with the other arm "claiming" the cabinet, and weight shifted to one leg. The woman on the left is leaning against the cabinet with center partially closed by her posture and low hand clasp; she is looking up. The secretary is standing stiffly with her center closed off by her clasped arms and slightly bent posture. She has her head in a somewhat submissive downward position.

The most important feature of this conversation is the position of the manager. The three subordinates form the corners of an equal-sided triangle with the manager looking in from the outside. Rather than forming a "choir," the group is oriented away from him. His neutral facial expression contrasts with the pleasant expressions of the others in conversation. Although he is in a dominant position, with hands in pocket and feet widely planted, he is still formally closed with his leaning stance. If you were dealing with this group, you should be alert for problems. It is possible that the manager is aloof or is not generating the respect he deserves with his three subordinates.

Another important feature of the conversation is the difference between the NVC of the two supervisors. While the woman on the left cannot comfortably (or with taste) assume the position of her male counterpart in the vest, she could stand in a more positive manner. The man is her competitor for advancement, and she should not emphasize any disadvantages such as height by leaning or slumping. Begin to watch the men and women in your organization for differences in their NVC.

In Chapter 1 you read the story of Joe B., the architect who could pick out the Star and Heel in any meeting. Figure 6–9 shows a small group listening to a presentation, including two of the people from Figure 6–8. Using the NVC information you have learned so far, try to answer the following questions:

1. Who is the most important person there?
2. Who is the least important?
3. Who is the second most important person?
4. Which one of the two VIPs is the Heel and which one is the Star?
5. Is there anything in the picture that helps you analyze the relationships in Figure 6–8?

If we label the participants Nos. 1–5 from the left, No. 4 appears to be the most important in the right-hand group. No. 5 sits stiffly with fixed gaze, and No. 3 appears to be intent on No. 5's reactions. On the basis of posture alone, No. 5 seems to be the least important. In the other pair, No. 2 is more relaxed and possibly more important. But these two have allowed themselves to be outnumbered and don't appear relaxed enough to offset the apparent show of strength from No. 4. No. 1 shows a more relaxed posture of higher status than either No. 3 or No. 5 and evidently (from his lean) has a good relationship with No. 2.

No. 2 appears to be friendly, and No. 4, the big boss, is the Heel. (Unlike in the Joe B. example given in Chapter 1, there is no "friendly Star," because the Star and the Heel are the same person in this case.) No. 2 is relaxed, upright in his chair, and alert. His center is open (notice the unbuttoned coat), and he has an evaluative tilt to his head. His feet are back under his chair in a readiness position.

This presentation is in serious trouble. The Heel has firmly closed off his center with buttoned vest, tightly crossed arms, and legs crossed away from the speaker (note only the right foot showing). His head is tilted back and away in a disagreement position. He also doesn't have his glasses on (note the glasses case in his jacket pocket), always a bad sign if he needs them for more than just reading. It can be like talking to someone with his hearing aid turned down. The final touch to this negative image is his retracted chin position, much like a turtle drawing back from his enemies. This man's mind will have to be sold over his live body!

A comparison of Figures 6–8 and 6–9 gives a clearer indication of the relationship between No. 2 and No. 3. As noted earlier, the woman works for No. 2, but she is obviously oriented to the Heel in the meeting. Both pictures reinforce the belief that there may be some problem between No. 2 and his subordinates, especially the woman supervisor.

Figure 6–8. Informal office conversation.

Figure 6–9. Executive meeting positions.

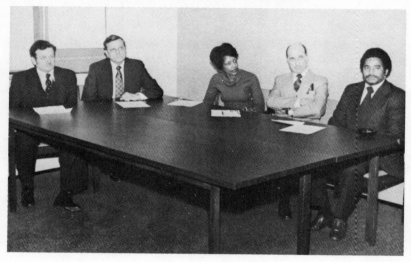

7

NVC and
Social Business

I had the opportunity to apply NVC under very unusual circumstances several years ago. I was sitting home alone one weekday evening when I received a phone call. It was my wife, who had gone shopping with a friend at the neighborhood market. In a plaintive voice she told me that her purse had just been snatched and that she would be home late. She was waiting for the police to arrive to gather all the pertinent facts.

My wife was much angrier when she finally got home. She and her friend had been pushing their carts out to the car when a teenager ran by and yanked my wife's purse off her arm. She did not have a good view of his face as he went by because of the darkness and the suddenness of the theft. Unthinkingly, she ran after him, only to see him jump in a running car and roar off with two friends. They did not turn their lights on until they were far away, so my wife could not read the license plate. What made my wife angry was that she had absolutely no information to give to the police when they questioned her.

Around two the next morning, we received a call from a juvenile bureau detective asking us to come down so that my wife could make an identification. "We've gotten a confession out of one of the accomplices and would like you to identify the one who took your purse," the detective said. My wife explained that she had no information, but he suggested we come anyway. As we waited at the station for the lineup to be arranged, I asked several questions about what we were going to do. In order to be legal, a lineup must place the suspect with at least three other people of the same race and general appearance. It would not have been acceptable, for example, for the young suspect to be lined up with a group of adults. The police found three other teenagers by putting out a radio call for squad cars to pick up any teenagers fitting the approximate description and bring them in. This point is important in understanding the mental state of the other members of the lineup.

After talking with the detective, we were ushered into a room where four suspects were standing on a stage with bright spotlights shining in their eyes. We sat behind a sheer black curtain so we could look at them unobserved. The first suspect, a short stubby blond, obviously did not fit the description. The other three looked very much alike and behaved in the following manner:

> SUSPECT No. 2 was clearly bored and resentful at being put through the inconvenience at 2:00 A.M. when he was "just out minding his own business." He turned insolently and stood with weight shifted on one leg, hands on hips. His head was tilted back as he rolled his eyes in disgust at each command.
>
> SUSPECT No. 3 was very matter of fact. He moved with no hesitation; his face was a relative blank. After a while he stood erect with hands clasped loosely in front of him.
>
> SUSPECT No. 4 was totally intimidated by the process. He stood slumped with head down. The detective repeatedly had to tell him to lift his head so we could see it. The suspect moved in leaden response to each command, squinting in the lights.

We left the room to confer with the detective. My wife told him she could not make a positive identification between No. 3 and No. 4. She did not want to jeopardize any young man's future with an erroneous ID. The detective then requested that she at least pick the one she thought was most likely the culprit:

> DETECTIVE: Could you make a guess as to which one you think it was? Although we probably can't use it in court, it could be another lever in questioning, since we already have broken down one of his buddies and he knows it.

WIFE: Well, if I had to guess, I'd say No. 4. I really don't remember the thief having a light mustache, but I might have missed it in the dark. Am I right?

COOPER: No, you're wrong, it had to be No. 3. (If you're going to stick your neck out, do it with confidence.) No. 4 couldn't have done it.

DETECTIVE: Yeah, your wife's wrong; it was No. 3. (Turning to me) Wait a minute, you weren't even there. How did you know who did it?

COOPER: Oh, I could just tell from their body language.

DETECTIVE: (Walking off) Oh, brother.

Although the NVC signs happened to work out well, it did have to be No. 3. What my wife took for guilt in No. 4 (head down and sunken-in center) was really submission. Here was someone who was obviously ashamed and humiliated at being dragged into a "real police lineup." This isn't the behavior of an intentional thief who kept lying to police until one of his friends broke under questioning.

What tipped me off to No. 3 was his lack of emotion. He was the only one under the lights who wasn't showing *something*. I can just imagine what went through his young mind. ("I won't show them a thing; I'll be a blank. They won't read me from the way I act.") But because everyone else had nothing to hide, his conspicuous poker NVC was the most damning evidence of all. When he unconsciously went into a modified closed center at the end of his movement, clasping his hands low in front of him (the only one to do this), I felt certain that he was the suspect.

I haven't had the opportunity to do any sustained research into the NVC characteristics of suspects in a lineup, but I find that my police officer students identify the suspect correctly whenever I use the example in a test. In two years I have had only one officer miss it, and that's because he wouldn't play his first hunch and erased his answer. Police officers are adept at reading people's behavior because it is their business. Their lives are often endangered in family disputes where anticipating people's actions can mean the difference between a calming chat and a brawl with family members.

Although picking out guilty suspects may not be a part of

your livelihood, there are many social situations where NVC can be of value in your career. The most common situation is the male–female ritual called courtship.

Courtship Behavior

I was standing in the noonday line of a downtown burger bar when I saw a fascinating encounter unfold. A young businessman ahead of me, looking to be fresh out of school, was lounging against the wall staring absently into space. I happened to see an attractive young woman notice him (I am always alert to what attractive women do strictly for NVC purposes) and walk over to where he stood. As she neared, she called his name and put on a dazzling smile. He started at the sound of his name, glanced over, and seeing the young woman, proceeded to change in a manner no less dramatic than Clark Kent turning into Superman after a brief visit to a phone booth. As his face displayed the eyebrow flash and smile of greeting, he seemed to grow in height and build before my eyes.

The woman was obviously taken with this new executive, for she stood in the classic "total rapture" position: listening to him from a close distance, standing erect with hands at her sides, and looking up directly into his eyes. They held these positions for several minutes as they conversed in animated fashion, then the woman turned and bounced off to her friends farther back in line. The young businessman watched her go with a smile, then slowly reversed his dynamic transformation, ending in the slumped position against the wall, looking like Lee Marvin's horse in *Cat Ballou.*

Courtship behavior of this type is not confined to men and women who have a dating interest in each other. It is usually indicative of general social interest, such as between a boss and a secretary or a male and female executive. One of the most common courtship indicators is self-touching or preening. Much like a bird smoothing his feathers (in birdland as in business, the males have large egos), we unconsciously arrange ourselves when we are expressing interest. As the young man above slowly stood up, he unthinkingly straightened his tie and hitched at his pants. The woman was in better control: she only smoothed her skirt three times.

There are many indicators of courtship behavior in addition to preening. The man will hold his head high in a proud and confident position, highlighting the neck and chin lines. The woman will give the corner-of-the-eye look made famous by those TV commercial lovelies who slither around in the front seat of a Mercury. The chest will be out and the stomach will be tensed or pulled in. If the woman is sitting, the legs will be in a sexy position, either crossed or with one leg tucked under. If she is standing, the feet will be placed in the model's T position, accentuating the curve of the hips down to a narrow base. In cases of extreme interest, there will be a pelvic tilt. The pelvic tilt rocks the hips forward at the pelvic bone, causing the back to arch slightly and accentuating the stomach and the derrière.

One of the best places to see these poses is in one of the higher-class girlie magazines like *Playboy* (which, as in the case of the young woman, I look at for purely academic purposes). Photographing a playmate is no simple business. It often involves several thousand photographs over a week or two, according to one Playmate of the Year. The poses, in addition to concentrating on obvious physical attributes, are carefully designed to create specific images. The poses fall into two main categories: the tigress and the kitten. The tigress has all the courtship indicators, giving a very aggressive impression for those readers who are attracted to aggressive women. The kitten shows few or none of these signs, often posing in a demure fashion of passive enticement.

It is easy to tell if a man is affected by live or pictorial female interest signs. Researchers found that a man's eyes will dilate when viewing sexually exciting material. A female will most often indicate her interest by showing her palms in feminine gestures—from holding the man's forearm as they converse to coughing coquettishly with the back of the hand to the mouth.

The limp wrist is also a positive sign of female interest. In my lectures, I joke that Sammy Davis, Jr. always sings with his hand away from the microphone limp at the wrist. He has to because of the weight of the diamonds. For some reason, men usually keep their wrists straight. A man will never bend his wrist as he walks arm in arm with his lady friend, but a woman will carry her purse through the office with the wrist limply dangling toward the floor. The more palming and bent-wrist gestures you see during a conversation, the more interest there may be (particularly if the gestures are being watched through dilated eyes).

Male courtship behavior is characterized by overlong gazes (immoral looking time), droopy eyelids, and a slight smile. When I illustrate immoral looking time to my audiences, the women usually blush and the men shift uncomfortably. A male courtship stance is usually fully upright or cockily shifted with the weight on one leg, like Snoopy leaning up against the school building as "Joe Cool." In either case, the chest is out, the stomach in, the chin tucked back, and the head tilted in a relaxed "agree" position. The hands are often held in a dominant and aggressive hip position or a modification with thumbs hooked in the belt or hands in pockets. As the publicity photos of John Travolta in *Saturday Night Fever* showed, pelvic tilt in a man is now acceptable. Every shot showed him in the haughty arched-back position.

At a distance, interest is revealed by smiling, preening, and immoral looking time, as the story in Chapter 4 about my friend looking at passing women showed. Close up, you can begin to spot NVC signs that often indicate more than just interest. A lovers' look, sometimes called a "knowing glance," passes between two people who are sharing intimacies. They may also have "lovers' hands," which break the touching barriers normally present in social situations. Their touch may last a fraction of a second too long, or they may touch normally forbidden areas such as shoulders in too familiar a manner. When more interesting essentials are made available after hours, lovers often forget that touching in the office is limited to obvious nonessentials.

It is also possible to manipulate courtship behavior. Remembering a prank from college days, one of my associates set up a special blind date with one of his friends and a man in our office. Before the date, he had a talk with the man:

ASSOCIATE: You're really going to like this gal. She's very attractive and a lot of fun on a date.

MAN: Okay, what is it? I knew there had to be some problem.

ASSOCIATE: Well, she had a slight accident with one eye as a child, and she's very sensitive about it because sometimes it doesn't track quite right.

MAN: Which eye is it?

ASSOCIATE: Oh, I don't remember, but you can tell if you look closely.

He then went to his friend and told her the same story: "He's really a great guy, but there is one problem that he's very sensitive about. His one eye doesn't track quite right at times, but you should pretend you don't notice." Of course he didn't remember which eye, but he was sure she would be able to tell if she looked closely.

You can imagine what the date was like. Although they had a good time with each other, they spent the entire evening staring raptly into each other's eyes, searching in vain for the "problem eye." With most practical jokes, humor is in the eye of the jokester and not the victim. Fortunately, both parties saw the humor in the situation; and since they had a good time with each other, they postponed the murder until a more convenient date.

I've seen this same trick pulled with each person being told that the other is "self-consciously deaf, so if your date speaks loud, you speak loud back." Couples end up yelling at each other all night, so beware!

Begin to notice the male–female interaction in your working environment (and socially too). NVC can be a good cross-check against the grapevine, and it is often more reliable. Even if you're not in the "pick-up" business, you can pick up on when there is more electricity in the air than in the walls.

Travel NVC

Unfortunately, we cannot spend all (or more) of our time talking to the opposite sex. One of the common requirements of business life is traveling, which is often dreaded and is normally just endured. Traveling is also one of the least comfortable activities of business, ranking right down there with riding in an elevator and getting fired. Flying, for example, consists of a sorry series of events lowlighted by the flight itself.

In a typical trip, you arrive at the airport and park your car in one of the long-term parking facilities conveniently located in the next county. You hike across the lot to the shuttle bus waiting area. If it's summer, the shade is well past the seats in the lean-to. If it's winter, the enclosure is facing *into* the wind. You stand with a group of strangers (or sit, with the metal seat conveying the subfreezing temperature to your posterior) as the biting wind whips over the level parking lot. You bump into the luggage littering the waiting area and stay as far away from other people as possible.

The bus finally arrives, a remnant of the local mass-transit system that the mechanics couldn't revive. You battle your way up the stairs with your luggage, banging knees and bus alike. As the bus fills, you breathe a sigh of relief: there are few enough riders that you won't have to share a seat with anyone else. To make certain, you pile your travel equipment next to you before you sit down. Your nose curls as you smell the stale odors of thousands of travelers before you, mixed with the fumes of a decaying diesel.

The bus is well designed for your NVC needs. Most of the seats face the front, so no one has to look anyone else in the face and worry about immoral looking time. The last seats to fill are the ones facing each other in the front of the bus. The designers, understanding that passengers in these seats must put their eyes somewhere, thoughtfully provided overhead slots for advertisements so people could gaze in moral relaxation. When the bus finally begins its short trip, you notice that the passengers have spaced themselves out as far away from one another as possible.

You clatter off the bus at the airport and walk over to the sidewalk baggage attendant for your airline. You stand around with a group of strangers waiting to give your possessions to another stranger and pay him for the privilege of handling your belongings. You watch your bags sink down to a lower level on the ever present conveyor belt, always an unsettling feeling. As you walk away, you say the traveler's prayer, "Please let them be there when I arrive!"

Once inside the airport, you are assailed by visual and aural stimuli—chattering voices, echoing footsteps, and an array of displays and signs. People are scurrying about in a single-minded attempt to make their flight. You locate your carrier and join the first of several lines. No one traveling alone talks in this line. Talking is left to families or business associates who are familiar enough with the procedures to be relaxed. If you strike up a conversation with anyone, you are viewed as a cross between Jack the Ripper and Mr. Hyde. Reaching the ticket agent, you are greeted with the cold warmness generated by an intensive airline training program tempered from thousands of uncommunicative travelers. You answer the obligatory questions in an uncharacteristic monotone—"Fine," "Chicago," "Nonsmoking"—and go to the waiting area to find a seat that is not surrounded by women and children. You sit back and warily eye the other passengers, hoping to get a plane seat far away from the colicky infant in the next row. Your sense of territorial space has taken a terrible beating, but this is only a hint of things to come in the airplane.

You're no ordinary passenger. You know a few travel tricks. You wait to board until the last minute, avoiding the lines through the electronic detection equipment and entering the plane when the aisles are fairly empty. You walk past the first-class seats in envy (your company's too cheap to go 1-C) to your slot back in the cattle car. Looking up at the row letters and numbers ("Now is 'A' aisle or window?"), you find your seat with a sinking feeling. Sitting next to you is a bulky, sweating piece of beef with arms splayed out over the rests on either side. The poor young man in the window seat is staring fixedly out the window, pressed up against the cold inner wall in discomfort.

You stow your gear top and bottom and plop down, cursing the airplane gremlin who always crosses the belts so that you wind up sitting on them. You squirm in your seat, carefully trying not to touch the overflowing neighbor as you retrieve the proper ends on the correct sides and buckle in. You unconsciously mouth the chief attendant's preflight litany as you sink deeper into your shell of discomfort. Fortunately, your immense companion follows the unwritten rule of grabbing only half the armrest and gives you the back part. You take what you can and slip your elbow into the slot, leaning out into the aisle slightly to keep the proper space. You become almost blind to what is next to you to make up for the lack of distance.

Your territorial space sensibilities are now totally at war.

Like your fellow passengers, you bore inward to create an artificial privacy. The plane is quiet; few conversations between strangers start. The drink cart finally comes rolling up. The airline, quick to take advantage of your need to relax, offers a wide range of liquid desensitizers. You are only mildly aware of the cart as it thumps your shoulder going by. As the drinks are delivered by a teetering attendant leaning over your seat, you realize once more that the aisle seat can have its price if the help is clumsy. As you sip your soothing brew, you suddenly find a rear stuck into your face as the attendant delivers the orders to those across the way. It's just your luck that it is the wrong-sex rear, so there's nothing of interest to contemplate.

Next comes the meal, an airline's version of McDonald's au gratin. Eating on an airplane is something like trying to go to the bathroom with a broken leg in a half-bath with sand-finish walls or making a phone call from a booth containing fighting storks. Your elbows flash like the Three Musketeers battling the Evil Cardinal's men. Even if you have traveled in comfort so far, you now feel totally violated. The meal trays are finally carted off and you just begin to relax again when the back of the seat in front of you comes crashing toward your lap. The weary executive in front has decided on a snore-filled nap. You twitch as the beefsteak next door bumps your knee every minute or so. You finish the flight by rereading the airline's back-patting magazine, the *Rickenbacker Skymaster*, and the French version of the sickie bag instructions.

The flight comes to a merciful end with the jolt of a four-point landing (two landing gears twice). As the plane rocks to a rest, the passengers jump out of their seats even though there is no place to stand. It is better to stand hunched under the overhead storage compartment than remain another minute in the seat. You move forward while the Texas-born flight attendant plastically parrots, "Bah, bah, bah" as you file out. Thinking of the supersonic needle-nosed sound monsters, you muse, "No wonder people are willing to pay three times as much for a ride that is twice as fast!"

You step out of the entry tunnel into the open gate area, really relaxing for the first time since you left your car in the windy lot. It is time to prepare yourself for the baggage gauntlet and hope that your prayers were answered. You pass a bathroom, which reminds you of a not yet critical need (flying seems to do that). Preferring to go on the side of the road rather than in the terminal or on the airplane, you decide to wait. You arrive at the baggage area only to hear a disembodied incoherent voice bubble, "Baggage from flight eye sifteer is now arriving at carousel psst." Passengers space themselves out around the baggage belt, still conscious of the pummeling their territorial space needs have undergone. Just when you are beginning to worry that your bag never made the flight, it appears—lop-eared from having been bounced off the baggage train coming in from the ramp.

Lugging your suitcase through a terminal that looks like it is inhabited by the same people you just left, you examine the new easy-to-read international hieroglyphics that pass for direction signs. Mistakenly finding the rental car area, then the hotel limo desk, you finally locate the taxi stand. You feel a certain surge of power and sense of class as you give the experienced traveler's sign of wanting a cab, raising the hand up casually to say, "Here I am." Unfortunately, there is no one around to see your casually experienced sign; the stand is empty. When a taxi finally arrives, it doesn't even have a roof light or an ad on the rear bumper. The sign on the side says, "Bill's Ride 'n' Pride."

The driver is Bill himself and is usually one of two personalities: Bob Barker or Calvin Coolidge. (Occasionally you will get Hanna-Barbera's Mumbles the Dog, who talks constantly but can't be understood.) Bob Barker regales you with the fascinating aspects of his city and expounds on any current event he happens to think of. All that's required on your part is to stay upright in your seat. (In some cases, you can fall over if you keep your eyes open.) Calvin drives wordlessly but looks at you in the mirror throughout the trip just to keep you loose. The only sound that breaks the monotony is the steady and all too frequent thud of the meter eating up your expense allowance. When you arrive, you give Calvin a good tip because you don't know what to expect if you don't and "it's not worth it with these cabby types."

You enter the antiseptic hotel lobby filled with chairs no one ever seems to sit in and walk to the registration desk. The hotel clerk greets you warmly from behind an imperious counter and acknowledges your status by asking you to confirm that you are alive and independently wealthy. After the forms are signed and witnessed by a consultant with eidetic memory, the key is laid on the counter tantalizingly out of your reach, to be whisked away by that ever present faceless nonperson, the bellboy. (Why he's called a boy when he's often 60 years old and rooming in the VA hospital I'll never know.)

You now get to join the bellboy on a fun trip in the elevator. Your bellboy is nice, so he doesn't try to start a conversation on the way up. He knows you are mad enough at having to tip him to run an elevator and decipher the room-numbering system, which is well indicated with signs on each floor so you can stumble in tipsy and still find your way up. When you arrive, he performs other specialized functions such as unlocking the door, turning on the lights, opening the door to the bathroom to see if there is one, and holding out his hand. At this point in your day, you pay him anything to leave. For the first time since you walked away from your car, you are truly alone and can relax.

As you can see, traveling is one uncomfortable NVC situation after another. Even when I know what to expect, I find travel at least a bother and often downright unpleasant. The negative effects of travel are caused by the inability to adjust to a rapidly changing physical environment inhabited by strangers. The participants all become nonpeople because of the tremendous volume flowing through the system. As hard as the airlines try to personalize their service with nametags for their attendants, brightly designed terminal gates, and giveaway magazines, the impersonal nature of the effort remains.

You can now make your travel more pleasant by analyzing what has been happening to you from an NVC standpoint. Once you understand that the sanctity of your territorial space will be violated for the duration of the trip, you will be much happier. Once you steel yourself to doing business with an array of nondescript strangers (who regard you as a stranger too), you will be much friendlier. Once you start recognizing the NVC information that others are transmitting, you will be much more knowledgeable.

Be more observant in the terminal. When you pass a bank of phone booths, look at the various people sitting or standing and see if you can tell who they are talking to, the way you did with the executive in Chapter 1. If there are benches lining the walls or out in the open, notice how people sit at them. As with all seating arrangements, there are dominant and submissive positions. The person sitting submissively on one end of a bench is saying, "See, you can have the other end of the bench and we won't invade each other's space." The person sitting challengingly in the middle is saying, "I dare you to sit on either side of me where there's not enough space for us to be apart." I once sat that way on a bench near a baggage conveyor during the airlines' pre-Christmas rush. There wasn't a seat to be found in the terminal, yet no one asked me to move. At the end of half an hour, I had made my point and was beginning to feel guilty because of all the people standing. When I left, two people immediately sat down, one at each end of the bench.

On the airplane, watch how the attendants behave. I often get the feeling that they are mentally "slopping the trough." They serve with a machinelike formality that makes the McDonald's clerk repeating cry of "May I help someone?" sound like a marriage proposal. Because attendants have to reach so much, their center is rarely opened to the passengers. They are always facing down the aisle. In addition, the seated passenger is in the awkward position of having to look over and up to the attendant with the protruding headrest bulge at his or her neck. Consequently, eye contact is brief at best. When dealing with attendants, call them by name (last name) and maintain strong eye contact. It will do wonders for your service.

Be aware of the person sitting next to you. He or she is probably as unenthusiastic as you are about the trip. Play the armrest game to win. If you are sitting next to a "rest hog," wait until he or she moves an arm and grab the entire rest, then hold it out of spite until your arm falls off in petrification just to see what the passenger does to retaliate. You may as well have some fun. If you are next to a knee bumper, bring your tray down and start writing, your elbow waggling partially over your neighbor's lap. Change positions often. For your fellow passengers, it's like traveling with a two-year-old. Sigh or make funny noises with your mouth. If you are reading a book, even if it is *Differential Calculus*, laugh out loud every page or so, smiling and shaking your head. It will drive your seating partner crazy.

If the nonpeople next to you show potential, try to involve them in conversation. If they don't want to talk, you will soon find out. I find that most travelers welcome conversation. I've passed some of my most interesting hours seated next to strangers on an airplane. The chances are that the person next to you will welcome a respite from the impersonality of the trip. Watching NVC can make your trip more interesting. Using NVC to change what happens on the trip can make it more pleasurable. The choice is yours.

Restaurant NVC

Another common locale for business dealings is the restaurant. I always prefer to entertain out rather than at home because the environment can be so much better controlled. It never fails that when I've got that important client relaxed and enjoying himself in my living room, the toilet backs up all over the bathroom floor or the dog goes into labor. One time my automatic garage door opener broke with a guest's car inside the garage. It took me nearly 45 minutes to dismantle the attachment from the door to the track. Another nice feature about entertaining out is that you can create the impression of high living at very little cost. You can live in a dump and drive a rust box, but if you own one good outfit you can entertain in style and never lose any social status. The only real negative is that you are no longer able to eat in privacy.

Whenever people eat in public, they pretend they have suddenly gone deaf in order to create the illusion of privacy. Even though a conversation easily carries to the next table, no one shows the slightest reaction to what is being said next door. If a group is particularly loud and boisterous, the other diners will begin glaring their disapproval at the disruption of their illusion.

If you are the one making loud conversation, be careful of loose talk. I was eating lunch once with a group of people from my office when the topic turned to one of our clients. As the client's name was mentioned in a derogatory fashion, my friend Sam nudged me and nodded toward a man at the other table who suddenly looked as if he had grown rabbit ears. He could have been an extra in the E.F. Hutton commercial ("When E.F. Hutton talks, people listen"). There was no way to warn the other salesman without alerting the interested listener, so we quickly shifted the conversation to another subject. On the way out we told the others what had happened and discussed the dangers of loose talk. It turned out that the salesman had been overheard by his customer's immediate superior who relayed the comment directly to the customer.

People often have a hard time pretending not to be listening. I once ate lunch in a customer's cafeteria and eavesdropped on the conversation next to me. A group of executives were reminiscing about a friend who had been transferred. The one story I had the worst trouble "ignoring" concerned an unusual experience this friend had at a downtown motel in a large city. He slept in the nude out of habit and, having a room to himself, saw no reason to change. Getting up in the middle of the night, he staggered to what he thought was the bathroom door, walked in, and turned around to relieve himself. What he saw shocked him. He was standing out in the brightly lit hall absolutely naked and locked out of his room.

At that point, many of us would have curled up into a fetal ball and started crying. This executive was famous for his iron will and control of every situation. Searching the deserted hall, he found an old newspaper and wrapped it around him, tearing it to hold together and leave his arms free. His modesty taken care of, he continued to search the hall for anything else that would be of help. Finding nothing, he resigned himself to going down to the lobby and getting a bellhop with a passkey. In triumph, he found a house phone in the elevator lobby on his floor and called the front desk. The phone was answered by a laughing room clerk who listened to the story patiently, then commented, "I know. We've been watching you on the security cameras for about 15 minutes now. A bellhop is on his way."

The table next to me was in an uproar as the executives retold their favorite story. I was sitting next to them, twitching up and down in my chair, choking on my food, and trying to remain stoically deaf. What made it worse was that they saw I was laughing and began to watch me pretend I wasn't listening.

The next time you are in a restaurant, observe the other

diners as they silently "interact" with their neighbors. People never really eat alone; they merely don't have anyone at their table to talk to.

Restaurant owners understand this privacy problem and arrange their facilities to minimize it. The first thing they do is darken the room. Just as a theater goes dark to allow you to lose track of the people sitting next to you, so the restaurant lowers its lights to enhance the illusion of privacy. It can be overdone, though. Some places are lit so dimly that you feel as if you are eating in a submarine con at night. You stumble through your food in relative secrecy and walk out into the bright daylight snowblind for five minutes. The best level of lighting is one that is as low as possible without making customers say, "Boy, it's sure dark in here!"

Some restaurant owners try to minimize rear fear in their layouts. The local quicky steak factory (I refuse to call it a restaurant) recently added about two miles of partitions to its dining room. I came off the line and felt like a rat starting the maze. At the end, if I was successful, I would be rewarded with an empty table. Even though the dividers eliminated most of the eye contact between tables, they did little to create a feeling of privacy. The tables had been jammed up next to the partitions to preserve the restaurant's seating capacity. Without the partitions, the tables had at least been several feet apart. Now the customers were so close that even a whisper carried past the chest-high divider. Partitions can't maintain sound privacy; they can only create physical separation.

The most common approach to sound privacy is to mask the restaurant sounds with music. Since restaurant owners do not want to waste expensive space on making people comfortable, they substitute an aural potpourri that acts like a pimple coverup. It doesn't make the blemish go away; it just makes it less noticeable. After several minutes, our marvelous brain adjusts itself to tune out all the nonessential sounds and begins to think there really is "quiet"—that is, except for the kitchen.

Wherever I go I seem to end up next to and facing the kitchen. In the event that area is mysteriously full, I am put next to the serving area, replete with spare supplies and dirty dishes. It amazes me that the same restaurant displaying Louis XV antiques will have wide swinging doors that show brief glimpses of sweating cooks retrieving half-done meat from the floor, throwing globs of salad into a bowl, and chewing on their nails. And the requisite for most kitchen help is that they be able to yell like Foghorn Leghorn, so that diners eating in elegant surroundings and atmosphere (defined as old furniture, darkness, and no Muzak franchise) hear snatches of kitchen conversation wafting past the swinging doors. Such exposure to the mechanics of feeding people can spoil even the most careful of efforts in the dining area.

Another factor that destroys privacy is people watching us eat. Many times, the worst offenders are the help. Some of the fancier restaurants will assign a busboy to each table so that the ashtray is whisked away while the ash is still drifting downward. The waiter will hover nearby looking for the merest flicker of an eyebrow or a head poised to rotate in search. This type of service can be annoying at best and stifling at worst. I may be oversensitive to it, but ever since I waited on tables in my college days I haven't been able to view restaurant employees as nonpeople. (My ears did not become plugged the minute my uniform went on, though. Much like standing in the elevator, I frequently heard interesting bits of conversation, mostly between male and female diners.) I don't enjoy a meal when I know each chew is being monitored by two or more sets of eager eyes.

Some restaurants compound the problem by locating the waiting area next to the dining room. This way, the clatter of hungry patrons looking at you like children peering through a pet store window becomes part of your "dining experience." I wonder if owners do this on purpose to speed the turnover, or if they are just careless. On a crowded weekend, you can feel like a depositer withdrawing savings during a bank run under the panicky eyes of those hoping to find money left when they get to the window. I would rather eat in the kitchen than near the reservations desk, hearing the poor hostess squeeze through the crowd and periodically shout, "Johnson party of two? Johnson party of two?"

If feeling like stuffed customer under glass isn't enough to make you speed through your meal, sitting on restaurant furniture probably will. A New York City diner called in a management consultant to help speed its turnover of lunchtime patrons, who tended to linger over their meals. The consultant suggested calling in an orthopedist to solve the problem. The owner took the advice, hired the doctor, followed the doctor's recommendations, and immediately nearly tripled the lunchtime business. What the doctor did was to redesign the seats so that they were comfortable for only about 20 minutes, the average eating time. Early arrivals cleared out before the noon rush and the noon arrivals were finished in time for a new group at 12:30.

In the better restaurants I have visited, comfortable sitting time usually ranges from 60 to 90 minutes. After that, the bottom begins telling the stomach that no matter how good the food and drinks are, it is leaving. Most restaurants prefer tables that are supported in the middle by a single pillar with a wide base. The pillar and base greatly restrict the legroom underneath the table, so that it is impossible for people over 5'8" to stretch out. An hour sitting upright or with the legs bent back under a chair is about all most people can endure before having to stand up. A trip to the bathroom is normally the only respite—unless you are leaving. The normal four-legged table support provides much more leg space, although it does reduce the seating options. (It also stops all those "excuse me's" generated when you step on the base thinking it is someone's foot.)

If you simply want to entertain in a restaurant, one with strong drinks and a quick bar is probably your best choice. If you hope to transact some business during the meal, you should follow several rules. Unless you plan to linger at your table, you had better complete most of your conversation before the food arrives. Once everyone starts eating, the conversation will come to a standstill. Another good reason to get down to business early is that before-dinner drinks dull things a bit. If you need the relaxation, fine. If you don't, you're going to get it anyway. After dinner, the body begins to slow down in accordance with nature's plan. The stomach steals blood from the brain for the digestive process. The combination of booze dumped into an empty stomach and digesting food makes Jack a pretty dull boy. Hit your topics while everyone is still mentally present.

Choose the restaurant with care by asking yourself the following questions:

1. Does it have barely adequate lighting for eating?
2. Does it have sight privacy from neighbors? help? bar patrons? people waiting?
3. Is there acceptable sound privacy for the subject matter to be discussed?
4. Can you be assured of a table away from the kitchen, serving area, busboy station, and reservations desk?
5. Is the help competent but not zealous?
6. Is the furniture comfortable for the length of time you plan to spend there?

Remember that people's impression of a restaurant is more often a result of the time they had there than of how good the food was. So only when all the above questions are answered satisfactorily should you worry about the food. Quality will often vary from dish to dish, night to night, and opinion to opinion. As the above questions suggest, you should never plan an important evening around a restaurant you have never been in. From an NVC standpoint, good restaurants are hard to find, so begin to analyze your favorites and any new places you encounter. It's time you got more out of a meal than a full belly.

Shopping NVC

I am always put off by the customer chaser masquerading as a clerk who says, "May I help you?" and then stands there while you look at the goods. I feel like Linus staring at Snoopy when he is playing vulture up in the tree by his house. I want to grab whatever I am looking at in one arm and start sucking my thumb. Salespeople don't really want to stand and watch customers either, or else they wouldn't ask a question that invites a "no." They're like children who come to your door saying, "You wouldn't really want any seeds today, would you?" When you agree, you can see the relief on the kid's faces as they begin to muster enough courage to go to the next house.

The problem, once again, is our difficulty in dealing with strangers. The rules of moral looking time tell us that we shouldn't be watched, yet the clerk wants to be of help (or stay close enough to make certain we don't cart anything off). We are nonpeople to each other, immediately placed under the headings of clerk and customer. Most of the conversation is very plastic, from the "May I help you?" to "No thank you, I'm just looking," to "Thank you and come again" at the end of the sale.

One retail store manager told me that the best way to break this pattern is to greet the customers as they come into the store. Instead of walking up to them after they have entered the store and asking the "help you" question, his clerks meet each customer at the door with a "Good morning" or "Isn't it a nice day?" They then *leave the customer alone* for several minutes, returning only when it is apparent the customer is looking for a specific item or needs some help. At this point, the clerks comment about the item or ask if they can be of assistance.

The manager also mentioned that the most important employee in the store is the cashier. Many stores make the mistake of placing an inexperienced clerk at the register or handling this step as a mass-production line. The position should be reserved for the brightest and most cheerful personality on the staff. The last person the customer deals with is the cashier. As the old saying goes, "You can have a bad meeting, but make sure the coffee's good so people can at least leave with a pleasant taste in their mouth." The cashier can ensure that any complaints are brought to the surface and that the customer leaves with a positive feeling.

The best retail stores have clerks who know how to be personal with customers. I once went with my wife to buy a dressy winter coat. We ended up in a small specialty shop that, in addition to women's fashions, sold the various antiques that made up the decor. The saleswoman, a native of Israel who was living in the United States, showed us how effective the personal approach could be. She introduced herself and within the first few minutes of conversation gently probed for all sorts of background information. She soon knew how many children we had, where we lived, and what I did for a living, and was getting a good idea of our personalities as my wife and I talked about coats. While my wife was in the back of the store looking at collars, the security guard in the front started discussing sports with me. My wife and I ended up spending nearly 90 minutes in the store, and by that time we were considering buying a hall tree, a cuckoo clock, and an English hunting horn, thanks to the skillful guidance of the saleswoman.

Managing to pin my right hand before it could get to my wallet, I began to think about what had been going on. I realized that the saleswoman and the guard had been treating us as friends, and that we felt incredibly comfortable with them. They had burst through the artificial barriers people erect for strangers, and in doing so had eliminated their own. We did buy the coat, and I'm sure we will shop in the store again, because at no time did we feel like the employees were hovering over us.

A local jewelry firm uses a somewhat different approach to break down normal sales barriers. All its stores are designed with the display cases about desk high. The stores are adequately staffed and equipped with small padded stools. When you stop at a counter to examine a piece, the clerk invites you to sit down and then unlocks the display case. (Even though you can't reach in, the lock is a good touch. "It must be valuable, it's locked.") This is an excellent selling approach, because it forces the customer to relax and gives the clerk more time to sell. Once customers are off their feet, they tend to stay a while. The clerks can service more than one customer at a time as long as they leave no more than one piece out at a time. Seated customers don't seem to mind being left alone as much as standing customers do. The cleverest part of the approach, though, is the use of stools rather than chairs. The stools are designed so that customers can take their weight off their feet, but they are not really comfortable. Like the seats in the New York diner, the stools ensure that turnover doesn't suffer by letting customers feel too much at ease.

Getting customers out of a store isn't really a major concern. Every retail store would love to have that problem. The important chore is to get them *into* the store. This is often done nonverbally with displays that customers see when walking by. The display must somehow say, "Buy me!" It must immediately catch the eye, and if the store is in a shopping center, it must be distinctive from other windows.

Most display windows are elevated so that the merchandise is at eye level. Within the store, goods placed on the upper shelves will sell better than those on the lower shelves. Just as we will write a phone number on the telephone booth wall at eye level, so we notice more when we don't have to look up or down. An old merchandising maxim states that "85 percent of the buy is in the eye." If a display can't catch the eye, it won't catch the sale.

We are also attracted by color. Displays using banners are consistently effective. Christmas windows are easy to do because the colors are bright and garish. Green mice in red stocking caps are perfectly acceptable at this time of year. Good displays involve the observer, encouraging shoppers to mentally put themselves into the scene. In fabrics, for example, where the goods anticipate the seasons by three to four months, a winter window will show a colorful spring scene, or a sunny day at the beach.

Once customers have been lured into the store by the display, advertising, or previous experience, the goal is to make them walk through the entire store. The layout can be cleverly designed to increase store touring. For example, the most expensive goods are usually placed in the front of the store. Most people will not want to spend that much money, but they will be impressed with the quality of the store and its merchandise. They will begin to work their way backward in search of more reasonably priced articles. The rear of the store is the best location for items in greatest demand. Display goods are placed here, because they will sell better than items not on display.

Specialty items should also be in the rear. For example, a fabric store that specializes in hard-to-find drapery material keeps these goods in the floor area farthest from the door. The manager explains, "We're noted for our fine selection of drapery goods, so there's no reason to try to draw people in with a display or to place the goods up front where they are more likely to be seen. My customers will go wherever the goods are located. If I had a basement in the store, I'd put the drapery goods there."

Sale goods require a different approach. Sale items are sometimes placed in the rear of the store, but more often they are spread out over the sales floor. Large discount stores and department stores often send out weekend flyers showing a wide range of goods. If you bought every item in the flyer, you would have to make a complete circuit of the store. These stores also move customers around with nightly specials announced on the PA system. Typically, the store first announces a temporary special in the rear of the store, then announces further short-term sale items located in the opposite corners. The announcement might blare out, "KC Store shoppers, there's a puce-light special over in the Sweatsocks Department. You can get pink argyle ankle wraps for $2.95 for the next ten minutes only." The announcer then cleverly never tells you exactly where the Sweatsocks Department is so that you have to wander around the store a bit. Store directories are usually vague for the same reason.

Another technique to make customers tour the store is to separate the entrance and exit areas. The entrance has a one-way gate so that customers cannot leave the way they came in. The only path out of the store is through the exit lanes, which are on a different wall from the entrance. Stores are also designed to make movement from floor to floor difficult. The elevators are buried in the back of some little-traveled department such as Scouting Clothes and labeled so that you can't see them from more than 20 feet away looking straight ahead. (This is frequently true of bathrooms too.) Escalators are often arranged so that you have to walk around to the other side to continue your way up or down. You are never allowed to walk adjacent to the elevator bank; your path is usually cut off by some department. Indirect pathways guide you past a number of the most interesting departments, such as women's sportswear and shoes. The specialty departments, where most purchases are planned, not impulse, are always located near the outside walls away from the escalators.

Departments are also arranged to fit customers' shopping patterns. Men's and women's departments are placed next to each other, so that if husbands become bored shopping with their wives (or vice versa), they can drift over to something that attracts their interest. For example, the local Target store places hardware next to housewares, and calculators and sporting goods next to cosmetics. All impulse items are placed near the checkout counters or the exit walkway (with a security guard stationed there to reduce shoplifting). All these techniques are designed to get you into other parts of the store.

Within the departments, there are many nonverbal tricks to help you make the decision to buy. One of them—called "pyramiding" in the liquor industry or "stack and sell" in the appliance industry—involves displaying an enormous number of items in a "sculptured" pile. The nonverbal message to many shoppers is that if the store had enough confidence to buy in such quantity, the items must be good. Another approach is to lay a large number of items directly on the floor, with a sign showing only the price. The informal display and lack of promotional hoopla suggest to the customer that the store is offering the items at a good price in order to get rid of them.

The layout within a department is also carefully planned to encourage you to buy. Good display space is never wasted on staple merchandise. Standard best-sellers can be relegated to the walls or placed on lower shelves, since these items do not have to be seen to be bought. In a grocery store, for example, people will go out of their way to find staple items such as soups and canned fruits. The ends of the aisles in any store are prime promotional spaces, because they are high-traffic areas. Customers pass them going up and down the aisles *and* walking from department to department. The most attractive, unusual, or colorful goods are placed here to lure customers over for a closer look. If a department does not have a particularly display-worthy group of goods, or if its merchandise is fairly stable (for example, small appliances), the goods are shuffled from location to location every week so that it appears, to regular customers, that new merchandise has been brought in.

Certain methods of display attract our attention. An executive for an appliance distributor told me that TVs are often displayed incorrectly. They should all be tuned to the same channel and left running with the sound off. As customers walk by the appliance department, they see a whole wall of images in synchronized motion, like a TV screen as seen through the lens of a fly.

Motion is the ideal attention getter. Paper flutters from the vent of an air conditioner. A humidifier runs off a clear plastic tank filled with goldfish; the blown moisture collects on a glass pane and is funneled into the tank below. All the clocks in the home furnishings section are set at a different time so that something is chiming, bonging, or cuckooing every few minutes. In shopping centers automobiles are displayed rotating on a turntable. The sign above the bank spins hypnotically, blinking time and temperature alternately.

Touch is another important attention getter. One of the advantages of running a TV with no sound is that a customer must touch the set to try it out. Once the customer adjusts the sound, a psychological barrier has crumbled and a strange sense of ownership begins to grow. You may pass by a car you test-drove once and still think of it as "your" car. You will search a counter for a ring you tried on several months ago before you look at the other items.

One very successful pet store owner depended heavily on touch in selling. Whenever a man and his son came in "just to look," he would leave them alone, watching the boy's eyes. When the boy spotted a pet, the owner would walk up and ask the father if he could help. The father would reply, "We were just thinking about getting a dog and wanted to see what you had." The owner would stride over to the puppy the boy was watching, get the dog, and hand it to the boy. He told me, "Once I get that puppy in the boy's arms, I'm home free. Most puppies will lick anything that moves. So there's the boy, with a squirming and licking puppy in his arms, looking at his father imploringly. It's almost impossible to resist. If the father is still unsure, I make *him* take the dog out of the boy's arms. I don't let him get away with, 'Now give the man the dog.' The boy glares at his dad and the puppy gets a shot at the father. If I can't close the sale 90 percent of the time when I let both people handle the animal, I'm in the wrong business."

Summary

A wealth of nonverbal information is being transmitted, received, and acted upon in almost every social situation. Observe and enjoy watching men and women play the "oldest game in the world." Be aware of the nonverbal environment when you travel and dine out. The next time you go shopping, notice which techniques the store is using to urge you to make the "buy" decision. There's an enormous amount of body business in social business.

8

Developing
an Effective Voice

As we saw in Chapter 1, words—the actual content of our messages—contribute only 10 percent to the communication of attitudes. In Chapters 2 through 7 we examined body movements and positions, which comprise 60 percent of attitude communication. It's now time to examine the remaining 30 percent: *voice*.

Voice is more important than many of us realize. Nixon found out that there was an immense difference between reading a transcript of a conversation and hearing a tape recording of the voices. We aren't aware of listening to a good voice because it gets the job done without calling attention to itself. Only when a voice is ineffective do we notice it. A good example is the "common person" or "celebrity" TV commercial. An immaculately dressed housewife "casually" being interviewed in a laundromat nervously drones, "I love new Green Sheen detergent. Since I started using it, my husband bought me a mink coat because he was so pleased with his underwear." Baseball star Stan Musial gallantly tries to promote the features of a shock absorber in a conversation with a sports announcer on radio. Musial is as out of the announcers' league as the announcer would be trying to take batting practice with "The Man" in an old-timer's game.

Some people make a living from their voice. Mel Blanc, the

actor who played Jack Benny's violin teacher and the Mexican visitor Si ("Sie? See, Sie!"), was the voice behind all the Warner Brothers cartoon characters. (In the movie *Bugs Bunny Superstar*, he talks about some of the voices he was asked to do. The most difficult was having to portray an English horse neighing.) Some actors have very effective voices for commercials. Paul Burke, William Conrad, James Garner, and David Janssen appear both on and off camera in many current TV commercials. The reason they are so much in demand is that they can control one of the most accurate indicators of feelings: their voice.

I use an exercise in my classes to illustrate the many meanings we can give one word with our voice. I invite three students to the front of the room and give them each a card with "Quiet" written on it, along with a description of how the word is to be said:

"Quiet!" (Be quiet!)
"Quiet?" (Is it finally quiet?)
"Quiet." (Sigh. At last it's quiet.)

The class has no trouble identifying the three different meanings of the word.

In addition to feelings, voice can indicate when we are lying. Inventor Allen Bell has developed a device that can determine whether people are telling the truth by analyzing their voice. Unlike the polygraph, the device does not have to be attached to the person. It can analyze tapes, TV transmissions, or phone conversations. Called the psychological stress evaluator (PSE), it measures certain tremors in the voice that are undetectable to the human ear. The voice produces a tremor at the rate of 8 to 14 cycles per second. When a person tells the truth, the muscles that control the voice are relaxed and produce a certain pattern. When a person lies, the effort creates stress and the pattern is altered. We seem to have no control over this process.

Bell first tested the PSE on the TV show *To Tell the Truth* (where three contestants claim to be the same person and the panel must determine which one is not lying). Bell claims the PSE was correct 95 percent of the time. In another trial, three PSE operators analyzed the statements of John Dean and John Mitchell in the televised Watergate hearings. Mitchell showed stress at several points in his testimony—for example, when he said he didn't think Richard Nixon had known about the break-in or cover-up. Dean did not show any stress. As we all know, history proved Dean right and Mitchell wrong.

Dale Carnegie, in his book *How to Develop Self-Confidence and Influence People by Public Speaking,* tells us that "we are evaluated and classified by four things in this world: by what we do, by how we look, by what we say, and by how we say it." You can improve "how you say it" by working on your voice. The muscles of the larynx can be strengthened and toned with practice.

When I first started consulting, I found it difficult to conduct a full day's class without losing my voice. I gradually strengthened my voice so I could do several days in a row with no problem. Getting greedy, I scheduled four days in succession one winter, two in Kansas City and two in St. Louis. Kansas City was in the throes of an ice storm, with the temperature hovering near zero. I was given a classroom next to the heating pipes, which banged with strain throughout the session. After two days of shouting over the pipes, I felt as if my throat had been dragged behind a horse, and I still had two days to go! In St. Louis, blessed with a quiet classroom, I managed to finish the two sessions without incident by using every technique I knew to project my voice with a minimum of effort. You too can develop control of your voice for strength, endurance, and effective public speaking.

Voice Control

We learn to control our voice at a very early age. Newborn babies can make thousands of separate and distinct sounds, but by the age of six months their range of sounds is usually restricted to their native language. English has approximately 50 sounds, each taking nearly .15 second. These sounds are made by a combination of breathing, phonation, resonance, and articulation.

Normal *breathing* is a regular cycle of inhalation and exhalation every three to five seconds. When we intend to speak, we inhale more quickly, then exhale in a controlled manner. Anyone who has played a wind instrument knows the importance of the diaphragm in good breath control. The diaphragm is a muscle between the chest cavity and the stomach. It expands, making more room in the chest cavity for air, and contracts, forcing air outward. Trumpeter Raphael Mendez had such breath control and mastery of his instrument that he could play *Flight of the Bumblebee* through twice on a single breath!

The air is passed into the windpipe and then the larnyx for *phonation*. Housed at the point of the Adam's apple are two vocal folds that produce sound. They are brought together and are set vibrating by the outgoing air. A set of incredibly complex muscles changes the length, mass, elasticity, and hardness of the folds to produce variations in pitch and loudness. The vibrating air is next passed to the nasal passages, throat, and mouth cavities to create resonance. This is similar to the function of the sound box of a speaker in a stereo system. The nasal passages and mouth cavities are of different sizes and shapes and are lined with membranes of different degrees of firmness and moisture content. The size and shape of most of these passages and cavities can be adjusted to modify the voice.

The final step in the speech process is *articulation*. We articulate by positioning our tongue, teeth, and lips properly for each sound. Many of us might say the last sentence, "We articalate by posishning are ton, teethe, and libs proply for eedge soun." This is simply being lazy with our verbal tools. One of the advantages of singing is that it teaches people to overarticulate sounds so that the audience will understand their lyrics. This discipline can carry over into everyday speech.

Dale Carnegie relates the story of a down-on-his-luck Englishman who was stranded in the United States with no money. He went for an interview in a worn suit and scruffy shoes, the only clothes he had. The interviewer was captivated by the man's mastery of the language. Despite his ragged appearance, his speech set him apart as someone special. Although the interviewer didn't hire the Englishman, he arranged for an interview with a business associate who did. By properly controlling your voice, you may affect people the same way.

Voice Codes

Certain sounds, like certain gestures, have universal meaning:

"Tsk! Tsk!"	Disapproval
Wolf whistle	Appreciation
"Augh!"	Frustration (Charlie Brown's cry when Lucy yanks the football away)
"Oops!"	Chagrin (whenever I miss a high pass in basketball I call it an "Alley Oops" play)
Bronx cheer	Derision
"Yea!"	Cheer; approval
Boo! (whistle in Europe)	Displeasure
"Ow! Ouch!"	Pain
Snort	Scorn
Laugh	Humor

Some words function solely as sound imitators—for example, *bang, pop, pow, wham, bop, boom, crash, thud, swish, swirl.* As small children, we used to orchestrate our play with appropriate sound effects from our all-purpose vocal noisemaker. Somehow as adults, we lose this versatility and uninhibitedness in using our voice. We become expressive only when we are emotional and can seldom rise to the occasion on purpose.

The more thought we give to our speech, the less expressive we become. With nervousness and anxiety, we increase our reliance on nonspeech sounds, called *nonfluencies.* The most common of these is the *er-ah-um-uh* family of sounds. When we are making a difficult speech, we unconsciously increase these sounds to give ourselves more thinking time. "Well, ah, there are several different approaches to busing in the large cities which rather, er, affect student performance."

Nonfluencies are often used to keep control of a conversation. As long as there is sound coming out of someone's mouth, it is impossible to say something without seeming to interrupt. Frequently, people will indicate that they wish to continue speaking by making one of these sounds while giving other NVC signs of conversation: head up, eye contact broken, the posture unchanged. A new salesperson trying to make all the sales points before the customer interrupts will try this.

We sometimes let meaningless phrases intrude into our speech. "Ya know" seems to be one of the most popular, particularly among young people and recent school graduates. "Well, ya know, engineers had to take nearly 18 hours a semester, ya know, so it was a lot harder to get out in four years than with another major. Ya know what I mean?" "Ya know" is one of the most insidious of nonfluencies. It's like yawning: once one person starts it, everyone is doing it. I once had a sales partner who was deeply into the "ya know" habit. In a few weeks, I said it as much as he did, as did our support reps and our boss.

Some people interject strange noises into their speech. One of my instructors in school would sip on his upper bridge as he breathed in. Another instructor had a strange "dh" sound that interrupted his sentences. "The next topic we'll cover, dh, is managerial planning." As we listen, we inject nonword verbal signals when we wish to speak. We clear our throat or "harumph" when we have something to say. We also clear our throat if we are getting into a sensitive area of conversation. "Did you have a nice time after the office party, Rhonda?" "Well, ahem, I did stay late and had a few drinks." In my classes I sometime have the students list and then read some of their long-term personal goals. They often read the more innocuous ones first, then signal the important ones coming up with an "ahem."

Other types of nonfluencies are repetition and omission. Repitition can take the form of a stutter or a repeated word. Porky Pig ends each cartoon with "Th-th-th-that's all, folks!" Or we may repeat a word: "I hope you can see—see what I mean." Sometimes we may repeat part of a sentence: "It seems that—it seems that there is no alternative." We can also omit part of a word, a full word, or an end of a sentence. Porky next stutters, "Let's go to di-di-di-di—supper." You may state, "It doesn't seem fair I should have to go!" Someone may reply, "The reason . . . you'll just have to."

Another type of nonfluency is the tongue slip. I once told a class I completed a project in "one swell foop." A student told me, "I haven't had much term this time." (I'm still amazed that no one has complained about cartoonist Gary Trudeau's rock star Jimmy Thudpucker in the Doonesbury comic strip.)

If you have a large number of nonfluencies in your speech, you are definitely hurting your credibility and persuasiveness. The problem with eliminating them is that like most people you are probably unaware of the habit, much as I was with the "ya know" pattern I picked up from my sales partner. What you can do is to set up your own biofeedback on nonfluencies. The brain is a closed-loop system. It can send control signals but depends on feedback from the controlled organs to make corrections. Researchers have found that the brain can control certain bodily functions that were once thought to be uncontrollable. For example, machines have been designed to provide feedback on blood pressure. A light blinking in time to a beep that corresponds to a person's blood pressure can be used to teach the brain to lower the readings.

The biofeedback system I designed to rid myself of nonfluencies revolved around my family. Every time I said "ya know" at home, my wife would quietly say my name.

"Well, Sue, it seems that, ya know—"

"Ken."

"Okay, it seems that Bill is going to be a hard man to convince, ya know?"

"Ken."

The mention of my name was enough to make me consciously aware of the habit. At first, my wife seemed to be doing nothing but saying my name every time I spoke. Even though I didn't have this "service" at work, I managed to rid myself of "ya know" in about three weeks. I then went to my partner and suggested he let me do the same for him. Although his dependence on the phrase was much more ingrained than mine, he too "cured" himself within a few weeks. Don't be afraid to enlist co-workers or customers in your biofeedback program. I've seen whole offices embark on "ya know-icide." It becomes particularly effective if you have to put a nickel or dime into the "ya know" box every time you use the phrase. Some groups have enjoyed a heavily funded "ya know" party from their fines.

Once you have reduced your nonfluencies, look for them to

creep back as you suffer withdrawal symptoms during pauses in your speech. Much like an ex-smoker wanting that after-coffee cigarette, you will want to fill up those gaps in your conversation with a sound, any sound. Tell your biofeedback partner to keep monitoring your speech for any irregularities. Once you have eliminated these undesirable speech patterns you can begin to develop good voice characteristics.

Qualities of Voice

The first voice quality is *pitch*. Every voice has a base pitch, usually described as high ("Hi, there, I'm Glen Campbell") to deep (William Conrad as radio's Matt Dillon). Our pitch changes direction with different types of sentences. Statements end with a drop in pitch and questions end with a rise in pitch. Say, "You've been working here for 12 years" as a statement and a question. One is a simple acknowledgment of fact; the other expresses disbelief that someone has 12 years of experience. The range of our pitch can be narrow or wide. Most Clint Eastwood characters use a monotone with little pitch variation; Radio's Great Gildersleeve used excessive pitch variation for a humorous effect.

Voice pitch can also be thin, tense, or throaty. A tense voice, produced by tightening the throat, is particularly difficult to listen to. I once heard a preacher who deliberately used a tense public-speaking voice in an effort to speak louder. After the first ten minutes of his sermon, the parishioners began to feel a tickle in their throat. Coughs of discomfort echoed through the sanctuary in sympathy for the minister's throat. Toward the end of the sermon, the listeners were offering a chorus of unconscious coughs and throat clearings in empathetic pain. The preacher was trying to speak louder in the wrong way.

Volume is the second voice quality. Varying volume to emphasize certain words is extremely useful in controlling meaning. Read the sentences below, saying the italicized words louder, and note the changes in meaning:

I should mow the front lawn. (I should do it rather than you.)

I *should* mow the front lawn. (I should mow rather than do something else.)

I should mow the *front* lawn. (I should mow the front rather than the back lawn.)

We can even manipulate what people hear by the way we say something. In my classes I use a collection of puzzles that I call a Misdirection Quiz to illustrate how the voice can control listeners. Two samples read:

1. How many animals of each species did Moses take aboard the ark?
2. When in history did California begin with a "c" and end with an "e"?

When I *say* them, though, I emphasize the following words (again shown in italics):

1. How many animals *of each species* did Moses take aboard the *ark?*
2. When in history did California *begin* with a "c" and *end* with an "e"?

As old as the Moses riddle is, nearly two-thirds of the class will miss it. One answer is, of course, that Moses never had an ark. The poor fellow, every time he tried to do something with water, it went bad on him or it dried up. Noah was the ark expert. The California riddle is tricky, and no one in my classes ever solves it. The answer is "always." Reread the sentence aloud, putting emphasis in this manner:

When in history did *California* begin with a *c* (pause) and *end* with an *e?*

California has always begun with a *C*, and *end* has always begun with an *e*. By changing the volume of your voice, you focused attention away from the alternate meaning of the sentence.

Volume is a good indicator of emotional intensity. Loud people are often thought to be forceful and aggressive. Have you ever tried to fight in a whisper? Right after we were married, my wife and I lived in a typical college matchbox apartment with paper-thin walls. Everyone could hear what the neighbors were doing and saying, particularly through the bathroom. We learned to argue in a forceful, angry whisper that more often than not resulted in our breaking up as we showed violent body language signs with whispering voices. When we moved to a duplex with greater sound privacy, we had a terrible time learning to argue in a loud voice. When we did, though, our disagreements were much more satisfying.

The proper way to produce volume is not to work harder, like the preacher, but to work more effectively. This comes as a result using the diaphragm properly. You don't have to run a large amount of air past your vocal cords to be loud. This makes you sound breathy, like a bubblehead sharing personal secrets with the world. You should push the air firmly out of your lungs with your diaphragm. My trumpet teacher would suddenly poke me there while I was playing a passage. If my diaphragm was pushing properly, I would make a slight gulp. If I was shoving air incorrectly through the horn, the gulp would become a blurp.

You can tell if you are using proper breath control with this experiment. As you speak loudly, loosely cover your mouth with your hand. If the sound is almost entirely muffled, you are too breathy. If the sound is only partially muffled, your diaphragm is pushing properly. Another test is to speak loudly without blowing out a match held several inches from your mouth. Volume is properly made with the larynx, a muscle that you can strengthen for louder and more sustained speech.

The third voice quality is *resonance*. Without it, the fullness of a resonant tone, the voice takes on a nasal quality that Dr. Bill Beeners of the Princeton speech department calls "the loveless twang."

Your resonant passages can be blocked by a cold or congestion. In our family, the proof of whether you had a cold was how you said "Pat Boone." If it came out "Bad Bood," you had a cold. You can consciously block off your resonant passages if you wish. Scuba divers learn to do this simply for survival. Most people breathe through their mouth and nose simultaneously out of habit. Under water without a facemask, this leads to choking and eventually drowning. So a diver is able to close off the nose when necessary.

As a hay fever sufferer, I often ran into the problem of having to give speeches when I was congested. I knew I sounded blocked a good portion of the time, especially in the summer. To solve this problem, I practiced my presentation on a tape recorder, using the scuba-diving trick to teach myself to speak without nasality.

When you have a cold, or if your voice sounds as if it is coming out of your adenoids, try one of the following techniques to improve your vocal image. First, speak more slowly and over-enunciate. I used to speak at normal speed or even faster when I was congested, because I tended to mumble with lack of reso-nance. When I felt I was speaking ridiculously slow and enunciat-ing as if I were a diction teacher, my voice sounded much more normal. Second, let the pitch of your voice play a more important role in your speech. Raise your base pitch a tone or two and increase your pitch range. This will help restore some of the expressiveness to your voice and will draw attention away from your clogged sinuses.

The final voice quality is *tempo*. We can speak quickly or slowly, fluidly or with hesitation. At one time or another in our careers, we have all been around the machine-gun talker. One of my favorite examples is James Cagney in the 1961 movie *One, Two, Three*. In this sophisticated Billy Wilder comedy, Cagney played a Coca-Cola executive in West Germany who continually spewed out numbered instructions to his subordinates. The pace is so fast that you must listen carefully to catch all the one-liners.

Radio comedians Bob and Ray have a routine where they parody *slow* speech with an interview of the head of a national slow-talking society. The "slow talker" speaks at the rate of about 30 to 40 words per minute instead of the normal 150 words per minute. As the conversation progresses, the interviewer be-comes more and more impatient, finally shifting in his chair in agony as he waits for the next word to drop. In my classes, I've found that speaking this slowly is third only to running my finger-nails across the blackboard and using squeaky felt tip markers in irritating the students.

Fluid, continuous speech is best illustrated by those TV hucksters who do a one-minute commercial without a breath. Usually they are selling something like the Fed 'n' Shredder, which "dices, splices, slices, spices, and ices nices twices. It will size, disguise, revise, resize, liquidize, gourmandize, oxidize, standardize, vitalize, equalize, sterilize, fractionize, tenderize, and pulverize anywise. And it costs only $11.95 with your check or money order, or $512.17 COD." After the address is repeated twice in another marathon sentence, you lean back in your easy chair exhausted from the blitz and breathing heavily as if you were pulling for the announcer to make it to the end.

You have also heard the typical pause-filled campaign speech delivered to a highly partisan crowd. The political analyst for station NACN (National American Columbian Network) comments at the close of the rousing speech, "Well, Frank, the mayor sure had the council in the palm of his hand." To which the anchorman replies, "Yes, Henry, in a ten-minute speech interrupted only 127 times by applause, Floral Oaks Mayor Harly Goodman announced his resignation."

Often, breaks in delivery can add drama to your speech or give emphasis to certain words, such as the "pause" in the California riddle. Taken to an extreme, these pauses, whether for thought or for effect, can greatly detract from your delivery. In my corporate training sessions, we retype an important speech an executive is planning to give (such as an investment broker's summary or a statement to the media) and break the speech up into the most effective voice patterns. President Carter frequently breaks up his sentences in unusual places, a trait that has not passed unnoticed by impressionists. A typical sentence might sound like this: "It is the right of the American people . . . to forgo certain . . . luxuries much . . . as I do. For example, . . . I don't see . . . Billy . . . as often as I should."

President Carter also has an unusual habit of letting his voice drop at the end of his phrases. This hurts his image of credibility and truthfulness (see Table 8–1). The regional manager I mentioned in Chapter 4 who smiled only with his mouth had this vocal trait. His voice merely reinforced his image of toughness and insincerity.

Table 8–1 lists different voice qualities and the images they evoke for men and women. The images are based on my research into the academic literature and on the results of experiments in voice technique. In my voice sessions, I have each student tell a short personal story that is tape-recorded and analyzed by the group. The table summarizes typical reactions to various qualities of voice.

Some voice qualities are open to more than one interpreta-

Table 8-1. Voice qualities and personality traits.

Quality	Male	Female
PITCH		
Base		
high	nervous, artistic,	feminine, emotional
deep	immature, forceful, mature, masculine	masculine, unemotional
Direction		
all up	nervous, high-strung	flighty, high-strung
all down	cold, unemotional, untruthful	cold, unintelligent
Range		
monotone	masculine, cold	masculine, cold
wide	dynamic, feminine, excitable	dynamic, outgoing
Quality		
thin	no significant traits	immature, sensitive, sense of humor
tense	old, stubborn	young, emotional, less intelligent
throaty	old, mature	unintelligent, cold
VOLUME		
Breathy	young, artistic	sexy, attractive, superficial
Soft	powerful	naive, emotional, feminine, attractive
Loud	aggressive, insensitive, boor	forceful, argumentative, masculine
RESONANCE		
Sonorous	healthy, energetic, proud	lively, outgoing
Nasal	many negative traits	many negative traits
Blocked	unintelligent, dull	unintelligent
TEMPO		
Speed		
Slow	careful, cold	unintelligent, lazy
Fast	outgoing, nervous, impatient	outgoing, nervous
Continuity		
Continuous	earnest, confident	confident
Broken	insincere, unsure	weak, uncertain

tion. For example, a soft voice in a man may be regarded as either weak and feminine or very powerful, depending on other factors. Marlon Brando used a quiet, hoarse voice in portraying the *Godfather.* Only men who command power and respect can afford to speak softly and slowly, making others strain to hear and wait for each word. Less authoritative men lose their presence and power by speaking with a soft voice. When a voice quality suggests two or more contradictory traits, only the most frequently cited trait (in this case, "powerful") is shown in Table 8–1.

Voice-Quality Combinations

The real benefit of studying voice qualities is that you can learn which combinations are effective in different situations. Research on this topic was conducted by asking actors to read the same script to an audience using different vocal traits. The listeners were then given questionnaires to evaluate the effectiveness of the messages. The experiment was modified and repeated several times with different audiences to verify the results.

Table 8–2 shows the best combination of voice qualities for projecting credibility, persuasiveness, and other traits. Pitch di-

Table 8-2. Effective vocal traits.

Trait	Base Pitch	Pitch Range	Base Volume	Volume Range	Speed	Continuity
Credibility	up	varying	up	wide	varying	less than normal
Persuasiveness	normal	varying	up	normal	faster than normal	more than normal
Cheerfulness	up	varying, mostly up	up	normal	faster than normal	normal
Satisfaction	normal	upward	normal	narrow	normal	normal
Warmth and Affection	down	slightly up	down	narrow	slower than normal	normal

rection, pitch quality, and resonance are not included in the table, since they do not change for any of the categories. Pitch direction should always be varied, rising and dropping for each type of sentence. A normal pitch quality is always desired, regardless of the situation, as is a fully resonant or sonorous voice.

I use the credibility voice for teaching and speaking. My base pitch is normally two full tones higher when I'm talking to a class than when I'm conversing during a break. I try to make my voice more expressive by using a wider pitch range. This is not only less monotonous for the students over a long period; it also makes me sound more involved. We tend to forget that what is "too much" in a conversation does not seem at all outlandish in front of even a small group. A higher base volume is also an aid in maintaining the listener's attention and reinforces the speaker's passion for a subject.

Increased volume also makes a speaker's soft range more effective. Billy Graham uses this contrast to perfection, following up thundering questions with a feather-soft rejoinder. Your tempo should remain varied. The best way to transmit credibility is to control the continuity of your speech. Well-placed pauses, together with appropriate body signals of evaluation and thought, show you to be a thinking, concerned, careful, and truthful speaker.

Contrary to what most of us think, persuasiveness is different from credibility. Although base volume should be higher for persuasive speech, pitch and volume range should be the same as in normal conversation. Persuasiveness is achieved primarily through the speed and fluidity of the message. The stereotype of the slick-tongued, fast-talking salesman is 100 percent accurate. We have all noticed TV or radio commercials that blare on after a quieter program. These loud commercials make no attempt to be credible through varied tempos and thoughtful pauses. Instead, they focus on being persuasive, bouncing the information off us faster than we can think. We see a bewildering array of characters soaking chalk in ink, ripping shirts in half, throwing their bleach away, or talking to each other through the medicine cabinet. All these unlikely events happen within 60 seconds, yet none of the characters misses a word.

Another useful vocal trait for business is cheerfulness. When

I first went into the real world as a neophyte marketeer, I asked one of the experienced men in our office what I needed to become a good salesman. He looked at me for a second and said, "A thick skin," then walked off. I soon learned what he meant: everybody loves to dump on the salesman, because he can't fight back. (A saleswoman still has it a little better in this respect, since chivalry is not yet dead.) On some days and in some situations, I don't feel particularly cheerful or salesy. But I know that I won't have a second chance to prove to a client or class that a poor performance was just an off day. I must always be "up." One way I do it is by psyching myself, like an athlete before a sports event. Another is by showing all the NVC signs of cheerfulness.

The cheerful voice uses a higher base pitch, with variations mostly in the upper range. The base volume should be louder and the tempo faster, with normal continuity. Volume should be within normal range. Table 8–2 also shows the best combination of voice qualities for projecting satisfaction, and warmth and affection.

Building Your Voice

Once you understand how voice qualities contribute to your image and to your effectiveness as a speaker, you can begin to change for the better. The first step to tape your voice. A low-cost cassette tape recorder can be of value here. Many businesses use them in their training sections, so you may even be able to borrow one for overnight use. Try to tape your voice when you are least aware of the recorder. Most of us become automatons when faced with a humming recorder, its reels spinning like pinwheels. Get a 120-minute cassette and leave the recorder on during a long phone conversation or during dinner when you can forget that it's running. Have a friend tape you while you are making a presentation or speaking at a meeting where there is frequent interaction. The important point is to get a record of your normal voice.

The next step is to rate your voice for the characteristics listed in Table 8–1. Also evaluate your diction. If you are working with a friend, rate each other's voice to get a better reading. We all are so self-conscious about how we sound that it is often difficult to be honest. Listen to your voice until it no longer sounds "horrible." I have heard myself enough times on tape to know what to expect, so I can now listen without pain. In a recent radio interview about one of my clients, I tried to use a lower pitch range. The adjustment gave my voice a more authoritative sound over the radio speaker. Before, I had always sounded a little high and nervous, although I wasn't *that* nervous!

The main problem for most of us is lack of expressiveness. We speak at a consistent volume, pitch, or tempo. There is a lot to be learned from the professional voices we are exposed to each day on radio and TV. Comedian George Carlin jokes that all the announcers sound as if they went to the same school of broadcasting. The reason they sound so much alike is that they have all mastered the techniques of effective speaking. My favorite place to work on vocal expressiveness is in the car (difficult if you are in a car pool). I have heard some commercials often enough to know them by heart, so I announce them right along with the broadcaster. I'll come home and give my children the news and weather report in *Sesame Street* style.

You should treat your voice as another body muscle. It too needs regular exercise to stay in shape. On my way to a customer seminar, I will warm my voice up by singing along with the radio, yelling at the other drivers, and thinking out loud. To the range of my voice, I sing falsetto along with my favorite records (for women, this is the "high soprano" voice) and thump the baseline to those pounding rhythm songs. I might spend a half-hour auto trip yelling my speech. Like any exercise, this is not to be overdone at the start. It took me many months before I could do four consecutive full-day sessions without losing my voice. If you feel a strain in your voice, stop.

Summary

Your voice is one of the most valuable NVC tools you possess. Begin to analyze the voices of other speakers and try to determine what makes them expressive or persuasive. Acquaint yourself with your own voice. It shouldn't be a stranger to you when you hear it, and it certainly should not make you wince. Then, much like a singer in training, extend your vocal capabilities through practice. For the first time, you will begin to manage the other 30 percent of NVC for your benefit.

9

Politics and Image

Most of us underestimate the importance of a good pro- fessional image. Politicians are one of the few groups to understand and control image successfully. Rarely is appearance such an important factor as in getting someone's vote. Americans are notorious for their emotional or illogical voting patterns, with candidates at the top of the ballot having a better chance of getting elected than those at the bottom. Americans also seem to shy away from the unusual. A candidate named Grableskew Hraboff is a longshot to win the alternate dogcatcher post. Adlai, Hubert, Wendell, Alf, and Strom have little chance against the likes of Harry, Jack, Dick, and Jimmy. A candidate who looks like he lives under a bridge and eats travelers will never get the nomination.

The importance of appearance was reinforced for me in the 1977 mayoral election in my home town. My family lawyer of many years was running for mayor on the Republican ticket (in a very Democratic community). He had received an impressive write-up in the largest local daily and was evidently well sup- ported by his party. When I mentioned his candidacy to one of my in-laws, she immediately asked, "Is he good-looking? I mean, what kind of image does he have?" She was not asking for her voting information; she was *assuming* that he needed a good image to have a chance at being elected. A good public image is now a prerequisite for success in politics. I doubt that someone like Abraham Lincoln could make it today. Who wants a Presi- dent who looks like the "before" in a Charles Atlas comic book advertisement?

Today TV plays a critical role in a presidential campaign. Imagine going into a TV debate that will influence an election in one of the most powerful countries in history. The office is one of the two or three most influential jobs in the world. It commands a mighty army. It serves over 200 million people. Running for the office is the result of countless lesser attainments, years of detailed planning. Few of us will ever face an event with as much personal career significance, where so much lies in the balance.

We blanch at the thought of lining up for a last putt that means $20,000. The idea of a $100,000 winner-take-all tennis match (even if the loser gets a "mere" $40,000 less) can freeze the most successful pro. But even these events pall in comparison with a presidential debate. The true effect of TV on a presidential election wasn't fully realized until after the 1960 Kennedy–Nixon debate.

The 1960 Kennedy–Nixon Debate

The 1960 presidential election pitted two experienced pros in a very tight race. Kennedy was the silver-spoon candidate, born to wealth and committed to public service. Nixon was the bootstrap candidate who fought his way to national prominence. Both understood the importance of the debate and worked hard to win it. But the results of the debate were startling to the American people and devastating to Nixon. A survey taken after the debate showed that people who *read* the transcript or *heard* it on radio felt it was a draw or gave Nixon a slight edge. But those who *saw* the candidates on TV—the vast majority of voters—felt the debate was a clear win for Kennedy.

A study asked the voters, "How did the candidates live up to your expectations for the debate?" The results showed that Kennedy and Nixon stayed even in being as concise, fair, and articulate as expected. But Kennedy was rated as more interesting, sharp, active, strong, colorful, handsome, relaxed, calm, deep, experienced, wise, and virile than expected. Nixon appeared more boring, dull, passive, old, weak, colorless, ugly, tense, agitated, shallow, inexperienced, foolish, and sterile. Yet both men were trying to maximize their appearance!

This debate has become one of the most highly studied media events in history. Its surprising results lie in a complex series of unfortunate circumstances, accidents, and misdirected strategies for Nixon, and some careful planning by Kennedy.

The campaigning before the debate had been difficult for Nixon. Because he was behind schedule, he spent the entire day of the debate speaking in Chicago before hostile Democratic crowds. In addition to fatigue, his health had been a problem. He had recently been ill, had lost weight, and was bothered by a knee injury. Kennedy, in comparison, had just completed a California campaign swing and was fit and rested. He spent the day of the debate in a hotel suite planning strategy with his advisers.

The TV producers did their best to guarantee the candidates equal treatment. New picture tubes were placed in all the cameras for clear, sharp transmission. A solid-color backdrop was provided to make the candidates stand out on the home screens. Small spotlights, called inky spots, were placed to shine in Nixon's eyes in order to eliminate the dark shadows caused by his heavy brows. The producers agreed not to show Nixon wiping sweat from his forehead, since that would make him appear worried or beaten. They also agreed to keep screen time as even as possible, so that neither candidate would benefit from a larger amount of exposure.

Nixon was concerned about how his beard would appear on TV screens. Nixon has light skin and a dark, heavy beard. Even though he shaved immediately before the debate, he still had a shadow. Many people have heard about the "makeup" Nixon wore that night. The truth is that Nixon used aftershave powder to hide the beard shadow from the TV cameras. This also came back to plague him.

Figure 9–1 shows the candidates as they appeared on the TV screen. I have used the appropriate NVC checklist items to highlight their appearance differences during the debate.

As you can see, Nixon's appearance suffered. Standing on one leg caused his coat to wrinkle and gap in front. His weight loss made his collar gap, and his clothes did not seem to fit properly. In addition, he did not show up as well as Kennedy on the home screens because of his lighter-colored suit. This was aggravated by the backdrop, which had been drying light even after

Figure 9–1. Kennedy–Nixon debate.

(From Randall P. Harrison, Beyond Words: An Introduction to Nonverbal Communication, *Englewood Cliffs, N.J.: Prentice-Hall, 1974, by permission)*

NVC Cue	Kennedy	Nixon
HEIGHT MIGHT	JFK was taller, although this was negated by the TV coverage.	RMN was slightly shorter, but this was not noticeable and had no effect.
SIZE PRIZE	JFK had a muscular body style. He looked healthy and fit and wore a well-tailored suit.	RMN looked tired and under normal weight. His suit fit looser than normal because of his recent illness.
HEAD	JFK shook his head as he listened, as if disagreeing with RMN's comments.	RMN unconsciously nodded his head as he listened, in apparent agreement.
Forehead	JFK had a narrow forehead.	RMN had a wider forehead due to his receding hairline.
Brows	JFK had "medially down-turned" brows, giving a concerned look to his face.	RMN had dark, thick brows, giving him a brooding, negative, frowning look.
Eyes	Heavy-lidded.	RMN had deep-set eyes, which caused dark shadows under his eyebrows.
Lips	JFK had a fuller, sensitive lower lip.	RMN had downturned lips, giving the impression of a frown; deep lines from nose to mouth corners accentuated his negative look.
Chin	JFK had a square, solid jaw.	RMN had a jowly chin, which was more noticeable when he spoke.
Skin	JFK was tanned from his West Coast campaign.	RMN was light-skinned; his beard showed in blotches despite the powder.
Hair	JFK had a softer, fluffy hairstyle.	RMN combed his hair straight back in a style close to the head; his hair shone.
POSTURE	JFK stood erect.	RMN leaned to one side.
HANDS	JFK used his hands when he spoke and took notes when sitting.	RMN gripped the podium tightly to help maintain balance when standing and sat holding his sore knee.
LEGS	JFK used an open stance, weight distributed evenly on both legs.	RMN stood on one leg, resting his knee, and crossed his legs when sitting.

repeated coats of paint. In fact, it was still wet at airtime. As expected, Nixon sweated heavily from the heat of the lights. Unfortunately, this caused his aftershave powder to streak, giving the "smeared makeup" look that became famous and accentuating his beard further.

The media precautions only increased Nixon's problems. The backdrop was just the beginning. The new camera tubes worked against Nixon since they picked up his streaked face clearly and transmitted it to millions of TV viewers. The inky spots didn't do their intended job either: they had been jostled out of line by news photographers milling about the stage before the debate began. Nixon still had those deep, sinister eye shadows the political cartoonists love. There was even one shot of Nixon wiping his brow, although it was from a distance.

Nixon also gave the impression of being in accord with Kennedy. Many of us unconsciously nod our head as we listen, as if to say, "I hear you." On TV, this made Nixon look as if he were *agreeing.* Kennedy shook his head "no" and took notes, supposedly to be used later. An exposure count showed that Kennedy was getting more shots and screen time than Nixon. Yet Kennedy's advisers griped about it to the director during the debate. Yes, *griped!* They complained, "Keep the camera on Nixon. Every time his face appears he loses votes." And he did lose votes. He lost enough votes to swing the election to Kennedy's favor, a result ranked as one of the major campaign blunders in recent history. Even though both men were trying to maximize their appearance and had enormous resources of talent and money to help them, only one was successful. In view of the NVC data being sent out by the candidates, it is little wonder that those who saw the debate felt so differently from listeners and readers. These lessons were not lost on later candidates.

The 1976 Carter–Ford Debates

The results of 1960 were on the minds of the two candidates in the 1976 election. When Jimmy Carter agreed to debate with Gerald Ford, many questioned Carter's wisdom because of the tremendous lead he held in the polls. But 1976 was a curious campaign year. Neither candidate generated much enthusiasm with the voters. Both were said to lack the personal charisma of a Kennedy or the political savvy of a Johnson. The issues were fuzzy in a down economy, and neither candidate was willing to risk being the first one to offer solutions. The arguments of "Why I was a good President" versus "Why I'll be a good President" excited no one. More than any other election since 1960, image alone may have decided the winner in 1976.

A Gallup poll conducted for *Newsweek* magazine asked 517 registered voters across the country who saw all or part of the second debate the following questions:

	Carter	Ford	Neither or Not Sure
All things considered, which man won the debate, Carter or Ford?	50%	27%	23%
Do the following statements apply more to Carter or to Ford?			
1. Seemed well prepared and well informed	42	38	20
2. Seemed nervous and unsure of himself	27	38	35
3. Would be honest and open with the public about his foreign policy	48	33	19
4. Would have good judgment in a time of international crisis	33	45	22

I believe the NVC information these two candidates transmitted in the debates explains the results of the poll and, ultimately, the choice Americans made for their President.

Neither candidate made Nixon's mistake of campaigning the day of the debate. Both prepared in detail in hotel rooms beforehand, memorizing tremendous amounts of information for the debate. Indeed, one of the main reasons each debate was limited to a single topic was to give the candidates this opportunity to stockpile information. We will never know how much of what they memorized was actually used.

Coming into the debates, each candidate had a carefully established image. Ford was the tall, rugged former athlete carrying the power and prestige of the presidency on his broad shoulders. The last two Presidents had aged terribly in office. Ford was the picture of good health after his first year. He was the only one of the previous three Presidents to leave office without being physically and emotionally drained. As the picture of Carter in Chapter 4 shows, Ford may be the only one of the last *four*.

One of my favorite pictures of Ford in office is the one taken when he received his injection during the ill-fated swine flu vaccination program. The picture showed Ford, sitting with shirt sleeve rolled and a needle going into his arm, smiling at the doctor. How many of us even *look* while we get a shot? How many more of us don't flinch? Although I don't know the exact circumstances, there probably were dozens of photographers standing around Ford as he received his shot, praying for the slightest show of discomfort. Then they could blast the embarrassing photo across the country. (Remember the famous Ford ski fall shown on national evening news one winter?) Surely the President of the United States can afford to have a pressure gun used for his injections. No, Ford showed he could defy fear and look a needle in the point, smiling. Whoever set up the swine flu shot knew how to make President Ford look tough.

Carter had a warmer and more sensitive image than Ford. Publicity photos showed him carrying his own clothes on trips, reading the Bible at Sunday school, lounging in blue jeans, and being interviewed in an open-collared shirt (as in the *Playboy* feature). Portraits by Avedon of both candidates when they were asked to pose standing show Ford stiffly upright while Carter is relaxed with one hand in his pocket.

Figure 9–2 shows four typical pictures from the second debate. I have once again used NVC checklist items to identify the different NVC information that the candidates transmitted:

Figure 9–2. Second Carter–Ford debate. *(Courtesy* Newsweek/ *Wally McNamee)*

NVC Cue	Carter	Ford
HEIGHT MIGHT	JEC is of average height.	GRF is four inches taller.
SIZE PRIZE	JEC is fit, with average build showing in a suit.	GRF, former football player, "could still hike the ball and fire off the line at Michigan."
CENTER	JEC kept his center open when talking and turned to Ford when listening.	GRF kept his center open when speaking and listened with closed center.
HEAD	JEC spoke with head tilted, "looking up" to camera; he listened with head tilted.	GRF spoke with head held straight and listened with head tilted away.
Forehead	JEC has normal-sized forehead and wears hair down over one side, a loose strand occasionally falling forward.	GRF has receding hairline, shows large forehead, and wears hair back.
Brows	JEC has bushy brows with vertical "concern wrinkles."	GRF has pale eyebrows, set close to eyes.
Eyes	JEC has wider eyes, outside corners turned down.	GRF has narrow, squinty eyes, often slitlike.
Lips	JEC has thicker lips, slightly downturned in resting position; prominent lines connect nose and mouth corners. He listened with slight smirk.	GRF has thin lips forming tight, level line in resting position; he has a toothy grin that could be interpreted as a grimace. He listened with a tight frown.
Chin	JEC has rounded, slightly jowly chin.	GRF has square jaw, that looks firmly set even at rest.
Skin	JEC's skin has a rough, almost grainy look.	GRF's skin seems smoother; fine wrinkles at jaw, around eyes, and along forehead.
Hair	JEC has coarser hair, arranged slightly over the ears; temples are silvered.	GRF wears his hair straight back in slick look; hair is off ears.
POSTURE	JEC looked more "back on his heels" than GRF. He stood upright but relaxed, and sat down when listening.	GRF looked "up on his toes." He always stood perfectly upright and squared to the podium.
HANDS	JEC held a pen in his right hand and rested it on the lectern; his left hand made palming gestures and rested on his leg when he listened.	GRF's left hand gripped the lectern tightly; his right hand made frequent gestures. He crossed his arms when listening, with hands open.

As the *Newsweek* poll showed, both candidates seemed equally well informed to viewers. Carter seemed much more confident. He also gave the impression of being more honest and open with the public about international policy, a sore point with the American people after the Nixon administration. But the viewers polled felt Ford would have better judgment in times of international crisis. Here was a tough man of positive action. As every football locker room says somewhere, "When the going gets tough, the tough get going."

Both men were well dressed. Neither made Nixon's mistake of wearing a suit that didn't show up properly against the backdrop. Their clothes were well tailored and performed perfectly. That is, they gave the candidates a professional image without drawing attention to themselves. I was teaching a public-speaking course at the time of the second debate. I asked my students to watch the debate and mentioned that I would quiz them on the delivery of the two men. One of the questions I asked was "What color suit and tie was each man wearing?" Not one student could answer, which is the ideal result.

Both candidates were also well prepared, almost too well prepared. Their delivery was about as off the cuff as a computer's. Much was made in the media about the time they spent in their hotel rooms before each debate, and about who came and went and what they said. This extensive preparation may have robbed each candidate of his spontaneity and image of conviction. At times the two seemed to be in a statistics duel.

In seeming honest and open, Carter had many advantages over Ford. Carter carried himself in a much more relaxed manner. He stood comfortably, sat when listening, kept his hands resting on the lectern, and kept his center open. Carter also has a more "human" face. His fluffier hair texture and style, bushy eyebrows, open eyes, thicker lips, rounder face, and coarser-looking skin help make him look people-oriented. He is also blessed with the Kennedy-shaped eyebrows of concern. His habitual hand movement—the preacher-style palming gesture—made him appear concerned, friendly, and relaxed.

Ford was very much the opposite. He was rigid and tight in his stance and never sat down, even during technical difficulties in the TV coverage. He made forceful edge-of-hand or pointing gestures. He closed his center off with his arms when listening and gripped the lectern tightly when speaking. His face showed strength of purpose and resolve. His combed-back hair emphasized his forehead. He stood with square jaw, lips compressed. Here was a man of resolve and action.

Both men also seemed to learn from the mistakes Nixon made while listening to Kennedy. Ford stood with shoulders facing Carter, head cocked in an evaluative listening pose, a slight frown on his face. Carter tried a much more dangerous strategy: the slight smile.

Political analysts had questioned Carter's wisdom in debating an incumbent, because of the limitations on criticizing. Carter could not show a lack of respect for the office of the President of the United States; nor could he be derisive. Instead, he used an understated smile that said, "The current President is doing it again. Let me just have my turn and I'll show people what's wrong with that." The smile conveyed an "I've got him now" or "He's playing right into my hands" attitude.

Whereas Ford showed with his pose that he was not in agreement with Carter, Carter showed disagreement plus the hint that he had a better answer. He looked *eager* to stand up for his rebuttal. Someone should have clued Ford in on his center. If he wanted to look truly negative, he shouldn't have turned toward Carter. Looking over his shoulder would have been much more effective.

Both men also adopted Kennedy's strategy of taking notes during the debate. Carter took notes in a normal manner, as Figure 9–2 shows, but Ford used a curious technique. Often he did not look down while he wrote. Very few people can take notes without looking at the paper. In my career I have met only one person who did this regularly, a personnel manager for a large company. She wanted to maintain eye contact with the prospective employee during the interview, so she developed the habit of writing things down in very large script, using an entire page for about five lines of information. This way she could write legibly without having to look at the paper.

Ford may also have developed this skill, but it was difficult to tell from the movement of the pen whether he was actually writing. Also, he never once looked down at his jottings during his rebuttal of Carter's remarks. It is possible that Ford was taking notes only for show, following instructions from his advisers. "Hey, Jerry, take notes, big guy. It worked for Kennedy and it looks good."

The *Newsweek* poll made it fairly clear what the American people were looking for in their President. Carter was declared the winner by nearly a two-to-one margin.

Ford might have been more successful if he had changed his style a bit to soften his image of physical strength and force. He could have made more use of a relaxed smile in publicity photos. Additional informal shots away from the White House would have helped him appear more like Mr. Average. It's too bad he didn't dig in his garden or play with model trains. He could have softened his gestures during the debate using fewer chopping motions. And he should have released his death grip on the lectern. This is one of the first habits to break in any beginning speaker.

Carter played the smile perfectly. No one was unhappy with his treatment of the President. He could have appeared stronger, at times standing up straighter and gesturing forcefully, with more edge-of-hand and pointing movements. It is not surprising that, two years into Carter's presidency, the major criticism of his administration was the perceived lack of direct, decisive leadership.

Both men hurt their image with their delivery. They spoke in slow, exaggerated tones, as if they were in front of 2,000 people at a political rally and needed to make up for the sound lag. Speaking before a TV camera is much like conversing from across the room. A TV speaker is really addressing people seated ten feet away in easy chairs. Ford and Carter should have backed off the public-speaking techniques and spoken on a more personal level. During the vice-presidential debate both Mondale and Dole used this personalized approach effectively.

You may never face a situation with as much at stake as a presidential candidate, but your image is just as important to your career. The first impression you create at a job interview is often the determining factor in an employer's hiring decision. As you progress in your organization, you have more time to establish yourself both through your accomplishments and through the image you project to others.

Building a Successful Image

An image is a difficult intangible to manage. You can't grab it, beat it, talk to it, or comfort it. You probably can't even get two people to agree on what your image—or anyone else's—is. So most likely you have no idea what kind of image you project, much less how to improve it. For that matter, do you even have an image? Do you have more than one image? Are they similar or do they conflict?

The first rule in successful image building is to be *consistent*. Nobody really likes the unexpected. What does your heart do when you are surprised? It gets mad! It beats in a sprint, pumping blood quickly through your body in case you have to take action. Let someone sneak up on you and startle you, and your muscles will briefly go into seizure, followed by your heart blowing its top. Even when the surprise is pleasant, your body goes through this process.

Management is a lot like your heart. It absolutely hates surprises. A manager once told me that he didn't care what kind of difficulties his people got into as long as he knew what was going to happen. What is known, even if unpleasant, can be managed. What is unknown can be grounds for dismissal.

For managers, the worst kind of subordinate is an inconsistent one. A good performer is rarely monitored; a poor performer is always monitored, and needs to be. In either case, management at least knows where it stands. But nothing is more annoying to a manager than having to check up on someone who might foul up and then discovering that the checking was needless. It's equally upsetting to have to deal with the inconsistent subordinate's personality. Is the subordinate going to be in a good mood today, or is there going to be fighting or tears?

The same is true of images. Most managers prefer employees whose personality traits can be easily identified. If a subordinate is very inconsistent, the manager becomes wary and guarded, fearful of a potential surprise. You have probably heard someone say of an associate, "He's a strange one; I just can't get a handle on him." This is worse than having negative personality traits. No one personality characteristic is inherently good or bad; its desirability depends on the job. What may be poor in a salesman may be of value in an office manager. If you have *no* obvious characteristics, management has no basis on which to judge you for any job.

Avoid surprises in building your image. Your image should be obvious as well as consistent. This way, the people who make the decisions that affect your career will have something to count on, something predictable. They can then pick and choose among the jobs that are best suited to your traits and that offer you and the company the best chance for success.

The next rule in image building is to make your traits *harmonious*. A businessman I know has a card that lists him as an office products salesman and a marriage counselor. (I've always wanted to have a card that read, "Dr. Ken Cooper, Neurosurgery and Janitorial Supplies.") It is very difficult to carry off a two-sided image—such as being hard-nosed with money but free-wheeling with ideas, or being a smooth talker but shy. The traits you choose to emphasize should agree with each other and fit together in a logical pattern.

People tend to think and talk in clichés, so the closer your image is to a stereotype, the easier it will be to establish that image. A personnel manager for a large chemical company claims she can always recognize one type of person by sight: the IBM office products salesperson. She feels they all look the same, talk the same, and act the same. It is unlikely that IBM is *that* good in selecting a certain type of person for its salesforce. (After all, their selection process *is* barely less intensive than that used by the Rockettes.) Still, the candidates selected quickly fit into a stereotyped pattern of what an IBM office products salesperson "should be."

Other stereotypes include the green-eyeshade accountant, the sliderule-carrying engineer (or is it a calculator now?), the backslapping yes-man, the pushy door-to-door salesman, and the shrinking-violet bookkeeper. These stereotypes are guaranteed to ring true in the minds of others.

If you want a nonstandard image, be careful to make your traits fit logically. In this case though, make certain that you don't come too close to a clichéd image, because that will undo all your efforts to be different. Many an office oddball has found that he is "just like Bob," even though the similarities are superficial. Make certain the cliché isn't still there working with you.

The most important rule in image building is to *be yourself.* As you grew up, you undoubtedly met people you admired and respected. You spent much of your time pretending to be these people and acting out their lives. As an adult, you must take your own talents and traits and maximize them, not try to acquire the traits you see in others. How many people do you know who are "wasted" in their current jobs or are trying to copy someone they are not?

Phonies are easy to spot. Today's young people are particularly adept at sizing up others. If we try to be something we are not, it will be incredibly obvious. If we really had enough talent to keep a fake image alive, we would be actors and actresses instead of businesspeople. Since we aren't entertainers, we had better stick to being ourselves.

That still gives us a lot of latitude. Everyone has many different personalities, with many different traits. Dr. John G. Geier, a consulting industrial psychologist, believes that managers have three separate personalities, defined by how they view themselves, how they feel others view them, and how they act under pressure. Each of these personalities has four major dimensions: dominance, influence, steadiness, and compliance. Geier developed a test to measure these traits in assessing a manager's style and effectiveness. His analysis may be overly restrictive in the personality traits considered, but it does illustrate our varied selves.

We may also have work, spouse, and parent personalities. In fact, we may have a separate personality for every role we play. One of my customers was a particularly hard man to deal with. He was secretive and continually kept me in the dark about what was happening in the account. Consequently, I was regularly surprising my boss with unsuspected problems. As I built up a picture of this customer as a paranoid, power-hungry sneak, I also began to learn about him outside of work. He was a warm, loving father and husband. He had many creative hobbies and was quite friendly and pleasant when he left work. He would have been a much better manager if he had let some of these traits carry over into his workday.

You are most likely the same way. You have many different personalities, depending on the environment and whom you are with. Sometimes your personality is mood-dependent: there is a "happy you" and a "down you." Out of these different selves is the making of a successful "you" that can be projected as your business image.

DEFINE YOUR IMAGE

The first step in building a successful image is to determine what your current image is. You may not be aware of your image, or you may think others don't have an image of you. You are wrong! Picture your friends and associates. As you think of a name, you suddenly get an image of that person. You could give a short summary of his or her personality traits. You may guess fairly accurately at how your friend would react to a certain situation or reply to a particular question. If you can do this with others, they certainly can do it with you. The challenge is to develop an accurate picture of yourself as others perceive you.

Many organizations use employee evaluation surveys to help managers get a handle on their image. One large corporation conducts training classes after managers have been on the job 3 months, and then again after 18 months. A detailed (and confidential) employee survey is used as a training and evaluation tool in both sessions with comparisons made between the survey results. This provides valuable feedback to the new managers.

The manager who is not offered such a program must do a little more detective work. You should start by finding out what traits you transmit to others and why you project these traits. You should be able to get a fair assessment from your spouse and close friends. Let them relay what people are saying about you. Frequently, secretaries are a good source of information, since they are often privy to conversations in the boss's office. Ask your manager what he or she thinks of you and why. This is a valid question and can provide valuable feedback on both your performance and your image. Be open-minded, and don't become defensive. Remember that the opinions expressed about you are *always* valid, if only because the other person feels that way.

Once you have an accurate picture of what others think of you, you can begin your self-analysis. In Chapter 3 you read about environment and physical appearance. You can now evaluate these two nonverbal indicators as if you were a presidential candidate designing or improving a public image.

Stand at the doorway of your office or work area and pretend you are seeing it for the first time. Systematically study it (this may actually *be* the first time). Look at it wall by wall, not missing a single paint chip or ceiling tile. What do you have on the walls—paintings, plaques, diplomas, nothing? Look at the furniture. What does it say about you? Is the office sloppy, or orderly, empty or cluttered, large or small? Where is the furniture located? If you had to draw a character sketch of the person who worked in this area, what would you say? Look at other people's offices or work areas in your company. What do they have in common? What sets them apart? How does yours fit in? In other words, what is your personal work environment telling others?

What about your office clothing? Even if you do not have the resources to modify your current wardrobe, you should at least become aware of how clothing contributes to your image. Does your clothing fit in with those around you? You don't have to become a fast-food clerk and show up every day in uniform, but you should know whether you are different or similar.

Is your wardrobe consistent? A salesman who was proud of his stylishness got caught one day with all his suits dirty or at the cleaners. So he pulled out an old one and wore it to work. That night, his wife came home and, seeing the suit in the wastebasket, asked what had happened. One of the salesman's customers, complimenting him on his taste in clothes, had remarked, "I really like your suit. It's almost as nice as what they're wearing *this* year."

Are you guilty of having a "wedding wardrobe"—something old, something new, something borrowed, something blue? If you are, you surely look like it. You don't have to keep up with fashion's every whim. But make sure your wardrobe says what you want it to say about you and that the statement is not conflicting.

Now is the time to look at yourself. You know how to analyze your body type. You should also analyze your face. What is its resting position? Are you frowning, neutral, or smiling? Aren't a large portion of the people you observe usually frowning slightly? Considering the amount of time your face spends in resting position, it is no wonder that this characteristic can strongly influence your image.

Another important part of your image is your attitude. One of the most basic of human needs is the need to be recognized. This is particularly true in the business world, where our feelings of self-worth so often depend on the feedback we receive from managers and associates. In transactional analysis (TA), the process of recognizing others is called *stroking*, and a unit of recognition is called a *stroke*.

There are positive strokes and negative strokes. Companies and organizations use awards to motivate their people ("M&M's" when the normal method, money, is not available). The training director of a large international organization talked about the problem of motivating leaders who held their posts for a single year. "We use an intricate series of awards," he said, "to overcome the motivational problems inherent in a short-term job. This keeps the leaders working throughout the year." These rewards are all forms of positive stroking.

On the personal level, positive strokes are like coat hangers: they tend to multiply without your noticing them. Suddenly, your whole day is full of good things to say to others and nice things being said in response. A retired executive, consulting with the Small Business Administration, was asked why so many of the companies requested him by name. "There are many secrets to success," he replied, "and I was fortunate to discover one of them early in my career. While I am no more competent than many of my associates, I always try to leave the other person glad to see me again, whether it's on the street or in the office."

The secretary of a college extension office was the opposite, a constant source of negative strokes. She always complained about her boss, the professors, and the working conditions. She couldn't understand why the people around her weren't more pleasant and cooperative. The most positive comment she could make was that someone had not been mean to her.

What if you were to carry a special notepad to work today? Each sheet would be divided into two columns: "plus" and "minus." For every positive stroke you gave others, you would make a mark in the plus column; for every negative stroke, you would place a mark in the minus column. Would your net score be above zero? If not, don't you think this is seriously affecting your image? If your score would be high in the plus column, could it be that you are a little too nice? Keep count one day, or one week, and find out how you rate.

By now you should have a better idea of what your image is. You must build a business image that is consistent, has harmonious traits, and fits your personality. In building this image, you should leave nothing to chance. Everything should be done for a reason.

Your next task in defining an image is to decide what traits you want to project. You may feel that you don't know enough about yourself to determine these traits. One way to find out is to take a battery of personality, interest, and aptitude tests. A number of psychological testing firms and consultants offer these services, but they are usually very expensive. Since many of the tests and testing procedures are standardized, you can often get similar services through an adult education course offered by a local high school. Costs vary, but they rarely exceed $50.

I went through one of these courses after I left college. The first night of the program, we were given a mental ability test and then a personality inventory survey. The second night, we took vocational interest and preference tests. The third night included discussing the test results with a counselor and selecting the aptitude tests we wanted to take to investigate our areas of interest. The fourth and fifth nights involved taking the tests and reviewing the results with the counselor. By the end of the course, we had a much better idea of our interests and abilities, particularly of how our abilities might stack up to others' in the business world. We also had a better idea of our personalities and of what motivated us. We were fortunate, of course, in having an experienced counselor to guide us, but the test results alone would have made the course worth the time and money. The information we gained was invaluable in helping us develop an image that fit our personalities and interests.

RATE YOUR TRAITS

Based on the data you now have about yourself, you can begin to determine traits you have that are beneficial in your current job. Table 9–1 lists 325 personality characteristics. Make several photocopies, then go through the list and circle about 50 adjectives you think accurately describe you. (There are many synonyms, so don't worry about getting every version of a specific trait. That will cause too much work later on in the process.)

Obviously, your self-analysis of personality traits will be somewhat biased. If you want to get a more accurate assessment and can remain nondefensive, have your spouse, boss, and associates rate your traits for you. Then compare the items appearing on their lists with your own. You might even take into consideration the characteristics that appeared more than once on your first-impression test (Chapter 3).

Now divide a sheet of paper into three columns labeled "helpful" (+), "nonessential" (0), "harmful" (−), as shown in Table 9–2. Go down your circled list of adjectives and place them in the proper column, according to how they affect your image and job success. When in doubt, place an item in either the helpful or harmful category rather than in the nonessential column. If you end up with all your traits in the helpful column, you aren't being truthful with yourself. Your plus-to-minus ratio can be as high as two to one, with the nonessential-column size varying depending on the person and the job. You now have one of the most useful tools for career success to come along since having a father who is company president. The three lists should show you what to emphasize in your personality and what to play down.

Keep in mind that the value of a given trait depends on the job. If you are looking to move upward in the company, you may want to make an additional list for the position you aspire to, especially if it involves very different success traits from those in your current job.

Table 9-1   Image traits.

absentminded	anxious	bitter	charming	conceited
active	apathetic	blustery	cheerful	condescending
adaptable	appreciative	boastful	civilized	confident
adventurous	argumentative	bossy	clear-thinking	confused
affected	arrogant	calm	clever	conscientious
affectionate	artistic	candid	coarse	conservative
aggressive	assertive	capable	cold	considerate
alert	attractive	careless	commonplace	consistent
aloof	autocratic	cautious	complaining	contented
ambitious	awkward	changeable	complicated	conventional
cool	defensive	dissatisfied	efficient	excitable
cooperative	deliberate	distant	egotistical	fair-minded
courageous	demanding	distractible	emotional	fastidious
cowardly	dependable	distrustful	energetic	fault-finding
critical	dependent	dominant	enterprising	fearful
cruel	despondent	dramatic	enthusiastic	feminine
curious	determined	dreamy	esthetic	fickle
cynical	dignified	dull	ethical	flirtatious
daring	discreet	easygoing	expressive	fluent
deceitful	disorderly	effeminate	evasive	foolish
forceful	gentle	headstrong	immature	inhibited
foresighted	gloomy	healthy	impatient	initiative
forgetful	good-looking	helpful	impulsive	insightful
forgiving	good-natured	high-strung	independent	intelligent
formal	greedy	honest	indifferent	interesting
frank	guilty	hostile	individualistic	interests narrow
friendly	handsome	humorous	industrious	interests wide
frivolous	hard-headed	hurried	infantile	intolerant
fussy	hard-hearted	idealistic	informal	introspective
generous	hasty	imaginative	ingenious	inventive
irresponsible	masculine	nagging	original	pessimistic
irritable	mature	natural	outgoing	philosophical
jolly	meek	negative	outspoken	planful
kind	methodical	nervous	painstaking	pleasant
lazy	mild	noisy	patient	pleasure-seeking
leisurely	mischievous	obliging	peaceable	poised
logical	moderate	obnoxious	peculiar	polished
loud	modest	opinionated	perceptive	powerful
loyal	moody	opportunistic	persevering	practical
mannerly	moralistic	optimistic	persistent	praising

One of the oddities of business is that people are sometimes judged more on their capabilities than on their performance.

Table 9-1. Image traits (cont.)

precise	quick	relaxed	rude	sensitive
prejudiced	quiet	reliable	sarcastic	sensuous
preoccupied	quitting	resentful	self-centered	sentimental
productive	rational	reserved	self-confident	serious
progressive	rattlebrained	resourceful	self-controlled	severe
protective	realistic	responsible	self-denying	sexy
prudish	reasonable	restless	self-pitying	shallow
pushy	rebellious	retiring	self-punishing	sharp-witted
quarrelsome	reckless	rigid	self-seeking	shiftless
queer	reflective	robust	selfish	showoff
shrewd	snobbish	stern	sympathetic	timid
shy	sociable	stingy	tactful	tolerant
silent	softhearted	stolid	tactless	touchy
simple	sophisticated	strong	talkative	tough
sincere	spendthrift	stubborn	temperamental	trusting
skeptical	spineless	submissive	tense	unaffected
slipshod	spontaneous	suggestible	thankless	unambitious
slow	spunky	sulky	thorough	unassuming
sly	stable	superstitious	thoughtful	uncomfortable
smug	steady	suspicious	thrifty	unconventional
undependable	uninhibited	unselfish	warm	wise
understanding	unintelligent	unstable	wary	withdrawn
unemotional	unkind	vindictive	weak	witty
unexcitable	unrealistic	versatile	whiny	worrying
unfriendly	unscrupulous	vulnerable	wholesome	zany

Someone management feels is a "comer" may be able to explain away poor performance as "the best in a bad situation." Selling this often depends upon how well the person's "next job" image is solidified in the eyes of management. These lists can provide you with guidelines for developing not only an image of competence in your current job but one indicating that you can do the next job as well.

PROJECT YOUR IMAGE

Now that you have a list of your desirable and undesirable traits, you are in a position to project the proper traits. This is the final and most difficult step in building a successful business image. Unfortunately, there is no well-defined system for imple-

Table 9-2. Sample image traits analysis for a specific job (corporate trainer).

Helpful (+)	Nonessential (0)	Harmful (−)
active	affectionate	absentminded
assertive	ambitious	aggressive
confident	candid	anxious
curious	conservative	argumentative
dominant	determined	bossy
energetic	efficient	demanding
enthusiastic	high-strung	forgetful
forceful	individualistic	fussy
good-natured	logical	hard-headed
humorous	methodical	impatient
informal	natural	nervous
intelligent	persistent	opinionated
interests wide	practical	reserved
inventive	sentimental	restless
original	simple	skeptical
perceptive	stable	stubborn
polished	stingy	tense
rational		worrying
self-confident		
showoff		
sincere		
thorough		
uninhibited		

menting your image. Just as no two people's lists will be the same, so no two people will use the same approach in projecting an image. You have been exposed to a large number of NVC signs and techniques, covering where you put your body and what you gather around it. You can now use this information to project your image.

Start with your work area or office. If you want to convey order and precision, have all material neatly filed and labeled. Keep an alphabetized phone pad with all pertinent numbers in it. Your desk should be neat, with the drawers carefully laid out for easy search and storage. Keep personal mementos to a minimum —for example, a single ornate three-part frame of family pictures. If you want to seem busy and productive, keep your desk covered with material, messages piled all around your phone. Have layers of file folders scattered about. Always appear to be hustling; walk quickly through the office even if you are going to get a candy bar. There are hundreds of possibilities, all of which are correct as they are *deliberate,* and convey some trait on your list.

Make your office work to your advantage. Arrange the furniture to best fit your space needs and to gain control over your visitors. Minimize any height disadvantage by adjusting the chairs or rearranging them. Design the layout to maximize your physical size. Make every decoration say something about you: your personality, your tastes, your interests, or your accomplishments.

Take stock of your physical characteristics. Should you lose a few pounds? Start exercising regularly, or take up a sport. When you get your next haircut, go to a good professional and describe what you are trying to accomplish with your appearance. Make every purchase of business clothing fit into your long-range plan and image. Know what you want from the start and let the salesperson help you find the right look. I can't say enough about the value of finding experienced professionals for these personal services. Even if they cost a little more, the advice they offer about style and physical appearance will more than justify the expense. We've all seen the TV experiment where a prominent designer or stylist takes a ragged member of the studio audience and returns the next week with a totally different person. That person could be you!

In his book *Winning Through Intimidation,* Robert Ringer details his methods of success in the income-producing real estate business. When he started out, he was like every other real estate agent, working for any commission he could get from his clients. After being shortchanged time and again, he decided to develop an image that would help him get every penny of the commission he had earned. Ringer developed an image that was so professional, so high level, that clients never thought of skipping out on commissions. He used an expensive book instead of a business card. He traveled with his own secretarial staff and sent his assistants by airplane to fetch any documents he needed. He even walked out on one deal involving hundreds of thousands of dollars in commissions rather than fall back on his old image and agree to less than he deserved.

I recently met a man who achieved success by developing the opposite kind of image. This man is one of the finest theater organists in the nation, but he has achieved national fame as a bumbling collector of antiques. You may have seen him on several network talk shows, displaying his oddball collection of vacuum sweepers, washing machines, and cooking utensils. What makes his visits entertaining is that these contraptions, much to his amazement and confusion, never seem to work properly. The character he presents is strictly a ruse, of course. In an interview on a local radio call-in show he mentioned that he never played the organ during his appearances. How could a confused, bumbling collector have the talent to make such beautiful music come out of an organ? That would totally destroy his image. So he confines his organ engagements to the city where he gained fame as a musician.

It is a constant source of amazement to me that the public can accept someone who says, "Goooollly, Sarjent! Ah jist cain't unnerstan' a thang yewr yellin' aht muhee," and then sings like a Metropolitan Opera star. Yet this is the power of an image in highly visible fields such as politics and show business.

But what about the business world? When I graduated from college, I was in a quandary about what personal business style to develop. I had accepted an offer for a position and had about two weeks to move, buy clothes, and report. A little research and questioning of people I knew revealed that the company had a conservative dress code. So I got a haircut and purchased three suits: dark green, dark blue, and dark brown. I bought five white shirts and seven striped ties that would intermix with the suits. With this dazzling array of drabness, I reported for work.

As I began my long and complex training, I could see myself fitting right into the mold. The clothing made me almost invisible, and the jargon and speech habits of the office were becoming ingrained in my conversation. People didn't work there; they were "on board." I began to think I had signed up for the Navy! My wife remarked on the change in me, not any of it necessarily bad, but a change nonetheless.

After completing almost ten months of training, I had to decide where I wanted to work in the office. Did I want to become a member of a large, well-paid marketing team, where I would be a junior member with reduced responsibility, or did I want to get my own sales territory and have complete control and responsibility for the results? There was another factor. Up to this point, I had been exactly like every other trainee who had come through the office. If I hoped to advance in this highly competitive company, what would I have to do to shed the invisibility I had thus far maintained?

After going through the psychological testing procedure described earlier, I felt ready to begin designing my image. No matter what else, I had to prove that I was different, and that being different made me exceptional. I turned down the lucrative marketing team offer and trained for the sales position, where I would have my own territory in several years. My hair grew back to a more comfortable length, longer than most men's in the office. In replacing my wardrobe, I tried to pick suits that were much less conservative but still businesslike. Eventually, I grew a mustache, one of the first in the office.

In a town that ardently supported the local football team, I stayed loyal to the Miami Dolphins, a team I had followed since living in Florida. My desk had Pogo and Ziggy cartoons taped to it instead of family pictures. I stayed clear of office politics and avoided after-work drinking parties. When one of my managers told me I didn't fit the mold, that I was an individualist, I knew I had succeeded.

I decided to emphasize my creativity. When my unit had to sponsor a meeting for the entire office, I stayed late one night taking pictures for a humorous opening for the meeting. I also volunteered to write promotion party and meeting skits for anyone in the office. While some of these skits took more time than anything my job required, I felt that late hours were worth the exposure.

I worked at developing a reputation as a good presenter. I spent extra time preparing and reworking my visuals and delivery. I taught evening classes at a local college in order to develop a "stage personality," and I let my manager know why I was doing it. While most salesmen dreaded being assigned any in-house presentations, I sought them out as an opportunity to shine to my superiors.

The results may not have been due entirely to image, but by my third year out of college I was earning my age (back before double-digit inflation) and had received my first title promotion, about two to three years ahead of the norm. And I was not the only one using this approach.

John C. had worked in our office for many years, but was an enigma. He was extremely well liked and competent, yet people knew very little about him outside of business. He had no outstanding characteristics or mannerisms; he had not been involved in any unusual events. When it came time to write a promotional skit for him, we were stumped, since we had so little information to work with. Then it finally hit us. His most outstanding characteristic was that he had no outstanding characteristics. We finally wrote a series of skits around that theme; "He's the only man who can walk into an empty room and it's still empty," "He's the only person that the personality meter doesn't have to be plugged in to rate." So everyone has traits that can contribute to a successful image.

Summary

You may not have the resources of a political candidate, but you do have the same requirements for success. Take a lesson from people who are professionals at gaining other people's confidence and commitment. Define your professional image. Identify and rate your personality traits, keeping in mind their relevance to your current job and potential future positions. Then make certain you consciously project your best traits.

You can be your own campaign manager, communications consultant, strategy expert, and planner at a mere fraction of the cost a candidate would pay for those services. After all, no one knows you better than yourself. Since you know who you are, you can now use your knowledge of NVC to let others know who you are too.

Selected Bibliography

Allport, Gordon W. *Becoming*. New Haven: Yale University Press, 1955.

Argyle, Michael, and Dean, Janet. "Eye Contact and Affiliation." *Sociometry* 28 (1965): 289–304.

Argyle, Michael. *Bodily Communication*. London: Methuen, 1975.

Beeners, William J. "Total Communications." Talk given to the IBM Marketing School, Endicott, N.Y., July 20, 1976.

Benthall, Jonathan, and Polhemus, Ted, eds. *The Body as a Medium for Expression*. London: Allen Lane, 1975.

Birdwhistell, Ray L. *Introduction to Kinesics*. Louisville: University of Louisville Press, 1952.

Birdwhistell, Ray L. *Kinesics and Context*. Philadelphia: University of Pennsylvania Press, 1970.

Condon, W. S., and Ogston, W. D. "Speech and Body Motion Synchrony of Speaker and Hearer." In D. L. Horton and J. J. Jenkins eds., *Perception of Language*, pp. 224–256. Columbus: Charles Merrill, 1971.

Davis, Flora. *Inside Intuition*. New York: Signet Books, 1975.

Davis, Martha. *Understanding Body Movement*. New York: Arno Press, 1972.

Darwin, Charles. *Expressions of the Emotions in Man and Animals*. Chicago: University of Chicago Press, 1965.

Dittmann, Allen T. "The Relationship Between Body Movements and Moods in Interviews." *Journal of Consulting Psychology* 26 (1962): 480.

Drillis, Rudolph. "Objective Recording and Biomechanics of Gait." *Annals of the New York Academy of Science* 74 (1958): 86–109.

Duncan, Starkey, Jr. "Nonverbal Communication." *Psychological Bulletin* 72 (1960): 118–137.

Eisenberg, A. M., and Smith, R. R., *Nonverbal Communications*. New York: Bobbs-Merrill, 1971.

Ekman, Paul, and Friesen, Wallace V. "The Repertoire of Nonverbal Behavior: Categories, Origins, Usage, and Coding." *Semiotica* 1 (1969): 49–98.

Fast, Julius. *Body Language*. New York: Pocket Books, 1971.

Fischer, Seymour. *Body Image and Personality*. New York: Dover, 1968.

Goffman, Erving. *Behavior in Public Places*. New York: Free Press, 1963.

Goffman, Erving. *Presentation of Self in Everyday Life*. New York: Doubleday, 1959.

Goffman, Erving. *Strategic Interaction*. Philadelphia: University of Pennsylvania Press, 1969.

Half, Robert. "Shorty in the Oval Office." Interview for the Associated Press, quoted in the *St. Louis Post-Dispatch*, December 11, 1976.

Hall, E. T. "Proxemics." *Current Anthropology* (1968): 83–108.

Hall, E. T. *The Hidden Dimension.* New York: Doubleday, 1966.

Hall, E. T. *The Silent Language.* New York: Premier Books, 1961.

Hare, A. Paul, and Bales, Robert F. "Seating Position and Small Group Interaction." *Sociometry* 26 (1963): 480–486.

Harrison, Randall P. *Beyond Words.* Englewood Cliffs, N.J.: Prentice-Hall, 1974.

Hinde, R. A. *Nonverbal Communication.* London: Cambridge University Press, 1972.

Humber, Thomas, ed., and Akeret, Robert U. *Photoanalysis.* New York: Pocket Books, 1975.

Key, Mary Ritchie. *Paralanguage and Kinesics.* Metuchen, N.J.: Scarecrow Press, 1975.

Knapp, Mark L. *Nonverbal Communications.* New York: Holt, Rinehart and Winston, 1972.

Korda, Michael. *Power.* New York: Ballantine Books, 1976.

Lorenz, Konrad. *On Aggression.* New York: Harcourt Brace Jovanovich, 1966.

Mehrabian, Albert. "Relationship of Attitude to Seated Posture, Orientation, and Distance." *Journal of Personality and Social Psychology* 10 (1968): 26–30.

Mehrabian, Albert. "Significance of Posture and Position in the Communication of Attitudes and Status Relationship." *Psychological Bulletin* 71 (1969): 359–372.

Molloy, John T. *Dress for Success.* New York: Warner Books, 1975.

Molloy, John T. *The Woman's Dress for Success Book.* Chicago: Follett, 1977.

Morris, A. R. *A Handbook of Nonverbal Group Exercises.* Springfield, Ill.: Thomas, 1975.

Nierenberg, Gerald I., and Calero, Henry H. *How to Read a Person Like a Book.* New York: Pocket Books, 1973.

Norum, Gary A., Russo, Nancy J., and Sommer, Robert. "Seating Patterns and Group Tasks." *Psychology in the Schools* 4: 276–280.

Pliner, Patricia, Kranes, Lester, and Alloway, Thomas, eds. *Nonverbal Communication of Aggression.* New York: Plenum, 1975.

Scheflen A. E. *Body Language and Social Order.* Englewood Cliffs, N.J.: Prentice-Hall, 1972.

Scheflen, A. E., ed. *How Behavior Means.* New York: Gordon and Breach, 1973.

Scheflen, A. E. "Quasi-Courtship Behavior in Psychological Therapy." *Psychiatry.* 28 (1965): 245–257.

Scheflen, A. E. "The Significance of Posture in Communication Systems." *Psychiatry* 27 (1964): 316–331.

Sommer, Robert. *Personal Space.* Englewood Cliffs, N.J.: Prentice-Hall, 1969.

Spiegel, John P. *Messages of the Body.* New York: Free Press, 1974.

Stanford, Phillip. "A Different Lie Detector—Your Voice Gives You Away." *Parade Magazine,* January 10, 1977.

Zunin, Leonard. *Contact: The First 4 Minutes.* Los Angeles: Nash, 1972.

Index

209

AMACOM Executive Books-Paperbacks

John D. Arnold	The Art of Decision Making: 7 Steps to Achieving More Effective Results	$6.95
Eugene J. Benge	Elements of Modern Management	$5.95
Dudley Bennett	TA and the Manager	$4.95
Warren Bennis	The Unconscious Conspiracy	$4.95
Don Berliner	Want a Job? Get Some Experience...	$5.95
Borst & Montana	Managing Nonprofit Organizations	$5.95
J. Douglas Brown	The Human Nature of Organizations	$3.95
Ronald D. Brown	From Selling to Managing	$4.95
Richard E. Byrd	A Guide to Personal Risk Taking	$4.95
Logan Cheek	Zero-Base Budgeting Comes of Age	$6.95
William A. Cohen	The Executive's Guide to Finding a Superior Job	$5.95
Richard R. Conarroe	Bravely, Bravely in Business	$8.95
Ken Cooper	Bodybusiness	$5.95
James J. Cribbin	Effective Managerial Leadership	$5.95
John D. Drake	Interviewing for Managers	$5.95
Sidney Edlund	There Is a Better Way to Sell	$5.95
Norman L. Enger	Management Standards for Developing Information Systems	$5.95
Figueroa & Winker	A Business Information Guidebook	$9.95
Saul W. Gellerman	Motivation and Productivity	$5.95
Roger A. Golde	Muddling Through	$5.95
Bernard Haldane	Career Satisfaction and Success	$3.95
Lois B. Hart	Moving Up! Women and Leadership	$6.95
Hart & Schleicher	A Conference and Workshop Planner's Manual	$15.95
Michael Hayes	Pay Yourself First: The High Beta/No-Load Way to Stock Market Profits	$6.95
Maurice R. Hecht	What Happens in Management	$7.95
Charles L. Hughes	Goal Setting	$4.95
John W. Humble	How to Manage By Objectives	$5.95
Jones & Trentin	Budgeting (rev. ed.)	$12.95
William H. Krause	How to Hire and Motivate Manufacturer's Representatives	$4.95